CHILDREN'S BOOKS TOO GOOD TO MISS

Children's Books
Too Good To Miss

REVISED AND ENLARGED
SEVENTH EDITION

MAY HILL ARBUTHNOT / MARGARET MARY CLARK
RUTH M. HADLOW / HARRIET G. LONG

12032

1979
University Press Books
Div. of UPBS, Inc.
302 Fifth Avenue
New York, New York 10001

To May, Margaret, and Harriet

Prepared by

May Hill Arbuthnot, former associate professor of education, Flora Stone Mather College of Western Reserve University; author of *Children and Books, Time for Poetry, Time for Fairy Tales, Time for True Tales and Almost True, The Arbuthnot Anthology,* and *Children's Reading in the Home*; co-author with Sheldon T. Root of *Time for Poetry*, 3d edition, and with Dorothy M. Broderick of *Time for Biography* and *Time for Stories of the Past and Present,* and of other books published by Scott, Foresman and Co.

In 1959 the Women's National Book Association awarded to Mrs. Arbuthnot the Constance Lindsay Skinner Medal for distinguished contribution to the field of books. Western Reserve University bestowed upon her the honorary degree of Doctor of Humane Letters, 1961, and in 1964 she was awarded the Regina Medal of the Catholic Library Association. In 1969 the May Hull Arbuthnot Honor Lectureship was established, based on an annual grant by Scott, Foresman and Co. and administered by the Association for Library Service to Children, American Library Association. The lectures are given in April of each year and are followed by publication.

Mrs. Arbuthnot died October 2, 1969.

Margaret Mary Clark, former head of the Lewis Carroll Room, Cleveland Public Library; lecturer in children's literature, Western Reserve University, 1945 to 1955; author of *Keeping Up With Children and Books,* published by Scott, Foresman and Co.; past chairman, Children's Services Division, American Library Association.

Ruth M. Hadlow, coordinator, Children's Services, Cleveland Public Library; past chairman of the Service to Children Round Table, Ohio Library Association; member of the Newbery–Caldecott Awards Committee, 1969–1970, and member of the Notable Children's Books Committee, 1976–1978, Association for Library Service to Children, American Library Association.

Harriet G. Long, professor emeritus, School of Library Science, Case Western Reserve University; author of *Rich the Treasure: Public Library Service to Children,* published by the American Library Association, and *Public Library Service to Children: Foundation and Development,* published by Scarecrow Press in 1970.

Foreword

If one man's meat is another man's poison, certainly one man's book may be another man's boredom. Nowhere are individual tastes more pronounced than in the field of reading. There is probably not a single book that a group of fifty adults would agree upon as a favorite, and the older the children the more nearly this is true of them also. The youngest might stand united in their devotion to *Mother Goose* and *Peter Rabbit*, but with older children there would be no such agreement. One child might put *Alice in Wonderland* at the top of his list of favorites while another would omit *Alice* entirely. Does this mean, if *Alice* is omitted from many lists, that we should no longer include *Alice* in our book offerings for children? Probably not, but it certainly does mean that we should scrutinize rather carefully the causes for its omission. Was it given to children when they were too young to be amused by its logical daftness, or when it was too difficult for them to read, or did they just miss exposure to *Alice* all along the way? Perhaps they would not have enjoyed *Alice* anyway; perhaps they were young realists with minds geared to science and machinery. But would they not have a chance of growing up to be better balanced human beings for having chuckled over Tweedledum and Tweedledee or the Mad Hatter's tea party?

This is a speculative question, of course, but there seem to be, in the great flood of children's books from the advent of *Alice in*

Wonderland, Tom Sawyer, and *Little Women,* certain timeless books whose appeal never diminishes. Some of these have become a part of our vocabularies, our codes of ethics, our standards of family life, our inner world of fancy, or fun, or sheer beauty. *Mother Goose, The Three Little Pigs, Millions of Cats, The Snow Queen, Heidi, The Jungle Books,* these and others constitute a literary heritage which we should not like children to miss, even though we realize that not every child will enjoy all of them. Nor should we expect them to. All we ask is that children be exposed to these choice books with the privilege of rejecting those they do not enjoy. Heaven forbid that any child should come to detest a good story or a delightful book of poetry because it was forced upon him. It will, however, be a rare child indeed who through the years does not develop some favorites among these fine books, provided he meets them at approximately the right time for him.

Lists of good books for children are almost as numerous as children, in spite of which there seem to be compelling reasons for this one. The first reason for this list is that the influx of new books for children is so staggering each year, and their pictorial appeal is so potent, that old favorites are being crowded out. The new books which replace them may not have equal significance. Age is no guarantee of excellence, nor are beautiful illustrations and recency any indication of triviality. There are plenty of old books for children which are much better forgotten and many new books of such unique and fresh distinction that they have about them all the earmarks of a classic except age. The question is, with new books inundating the bookshelves, who has time to remember that every generation of children revels in *The Tale of Peter Rabbit* and *The Adventures of Robin Hood*? Who is going to see that each new crop of children has a chance to encounter these old favorites at the right age? Who has time to scan critically the masses of new books and to watch, over a period of years, the children's responses to them in order to determine which of the hundreds seem likely to make the list of permanent favorites for a large number—never all—but a large number of children?

Teachers and children's librarians are in a strategic position to perform these services, and for this reason a group of us, whose work involves both children and children's books, became actively interested in the problem of determining which books every child should at least have a look at. We asked ourselves, first, which of the old books, the so-called children's classics, should each new generation of children be exposed to and at approximately what age? Second, which of the recent books show signs of possessing not only literary distinction but permanent child appeal? Rereading books for children over a period of several years, we weighed them for certain qualities.

First, we asked, *is the book good literature*?

That is, does the text stand up of itself, regardless of illustrations? Has it distinction of theme and style?

To answer this question we read aloud certain debatable books. Some of our favorites we discovered were pictorial lyrics but textual monotones. In short, the illustrations were carrying the story. On the other hand, we found many a text, *Ferdinand,* for instance, or *The Little House*, equally good without their charming pictures. This experiment of reading a story without showing the pictures was sometimes tried with children. In Wanda Gag's *Millions of Cats*, for instance, the pictures are small and not easily seen in a large group of children, but it was found that the story captivates them just the same. We admit that this standard of literary quality is subjective, but we are trained workers in this field, and recognizing the fact that specialists in any field—literature or medicine—do disagree, we tried to be reasonable. We listened to opposed points of view, we evaluated them and then re-evaluated books after a lapse of time, and finally we accepted a majority vote after all opinion and all records had been considered.

Second, we asked, *does the book make a significant contribution to the child's wisdom, or merriment, or appreciation of beauty*?

Some books broaden a child's horizons, give him new sympathies and understanding, open his insight into human relationships. Most good stories provide him with clear standards of right and wrong, show him the conflicts and ethics of human behavior.

Other books provoke spontaneous and wholesome laughter. Still other books, especially books of poetry, have the power of opening a child's eyes to the wonder and beauty of the world.

To determine whether a book has the power to perform any or several of these services, we considered records of home, public library, and classroom discussions; children's spontaneous responses to a book; their requests to have it again or to talk about it; the questions it provoked; the children's subsequent references to it, or their indifference. We also considered the testimonial of adults concerning their own responses to certain books read or listened to in childhood and still enjoyed in retrospect. Such books we ourselves reread and tried again with children. The recent books in the list are not too recent. Most of them have been acclaimed by large numbers of children over a period of at least two or three years. They have also been praised by numerous experts in the field of children's literature. While this is not an inclusive list, it is, we think, a wholesome balance between the old and the new, as well as an interesting cross section of different types of children's literature: fiction, poetry, biography. We have made no attempt to evaluate informational books in any field.

Finally, we asked, *does the book have child appeal?*

This appeal may be obvious and instantaneous, upon first reading or hearing, or its hold on the children may develop slowly, only after several hearings.

This last point is so important and so continuously overlooked that we need to consider it in relation to the whole list.

Some stories and some verses make a quick appeal just as some popular music does. Such literature includes excellent materials and others which are trivial and banal. On the other hand, certain stories and poems must be heard repeatedly before the pattern or significance of the whole can be appreciated. The fact that complete enjoyment of a book is slow in arriving does not mean that it is not worth struggling for. Rather, we should remember the patient assistance the schools give children in the development of a taste for symphonic music. It takes time, but if even a few children are carried from a limited enjoyment of only the most obvious popular tunes to a life-long ability to enjoy great music, it is well worth all of the effort involved. The same process is needed with some literature. All poetry, beyond the lightest of light verse, and such examples of exquisite prose as Kenneth Grahame's *Wind in the Willows*, must be heard and heard again, lived with, mulled over, and savored slowly to be appreciated. Yet most children, who would not have the patience or the imagination to discover such literature for themselves, enjoy fine poetry when it is read to them unaffectedly and well, and a child or two in every group will probably love *Wind in the Willows* as long as he lives if it has been read aloud to him by someone who loves it too.

To judge, then, the child-appeal of books, we consulted various sources. We scanned library records of children's voluntary withdrawals of books. Those topping such records in several cities would seem to be favorites. Whether or not they were good literature was another matter. We looked at the listings of books in such bibliographies as those made by the *American Library Association, The Association for Childhood Education, National Council of Teachers of English,* and *School Library Journal, Junior Libraries, The Horn Book,* and the *Bulletin of the Center for Children's Books,* University of Chicago. We used teachers' records of children's favorite books throughout our large public school system, and we consulted gifted storytellers in schools and libraries concerning the children's responses to and requests for stories and poems.

Nevertheless, in spite of our conscientious efforts to use available data from as many different sources as possible, this list does not represent a statistical research for children's favorite reading. It represents the judgment of a group of specialists, working with children and children's books over a considerable period of years, trying to determine which of the old books should be salvaged because of their rich significance for children today and which, out of the multiplicity of new books, should be cherished for the same reasons. This means, of necessity, a somewhat subjective rating of these books.

This list is brief. You will miss some of your favorites, but even as it stands not every child is going to enjoy every one of these books. All we are trying to suggest is that here is an irreducible minimum of books which every child should be exposed to and helped to enjoy. If he rejects some of them, that is his privilege. At least we are giving him a chance to see and hear fine literature, to browse around, to select and reject on his own. Some of these books, discovered in childhood, will be cherished always. In some of them a child will find laughter, in others heroism, beauty, dreams. If some children never develop the capacity to enjoy fine books, the list will still be worthwhile if it helps other children to discover literature they might have missed, literature

xiii

which opens their eyes to the joy of reading, to the power and glory of books.

May Hill Arbuthnot

Preface to New Edition

It is time for a revision of this list because some of the recommended books are now out of print and some new books have deserved inclusion.

The basic philosophy and approach of this list as stated by Mrs. Arbuthnot still hold true. Again books were reread; children's reading choices were checked; bibliographies were consulted; changes in social patterns were considered; and books were discussed with librarians, teachers, and parents.

The list is brief and, indeed, some favorites will be missed. It is, like the earlier editions, somewhat idiosyncratic; however, it is offered with the sincere hope that it will broaden and deepen the reading pleasures of many children.

RUTH M. HADLOW

Children's Book Awards

THE CALDECOTT MEDAL

The Caldecott Medal is named in honor of Randolph Caldecott, an English artist who pioneered in book illustrations for young children between 1878 and 1885. It has been given annually since 1938 to the artist of the most distinguished American picture book for children published in the United States during the preceding year.

THE NEWBERY MEDAL

The Newbery Medal is named in honor of John Newbery, a London bookseller of the eighteenth century. It has been given annually since 1922 to the author of the most distinguished contribution to American literature for children published during the preceding year.

Both medals were originally donated by Frederic G. Melcher (1879–1963). Since Mr. Melcher's death, they have been provided by Daniel Melcher, son of the original donor.

The awards are made each year by the Association for Library Service to Children, the American Library Association.

Contents

CHILDREN'S BOOKS TOO GOOD TO MISS

For Children Under 6

PICTURE BOOKS

1. LITTLE TIM AND THE BRAVE SEA CAPTAIN

Oxford Univ. Press

Edward Ardizzone
Illustrated by the author

A large book about the large adventures of a small boy! How Tim goes to sea, weathers a wreck, and comes home in triumph is told with a casual air that is entirely convincing. Fine sea pictures add to the unusual qualities of an excellent story.

2. MADELINE

Viking

Ludwig Bemelmans
Illustrated by the author

Life in a Paris school for little girls follows a pleasant pattern, and there is calm and security within its vine-clad walls until one night small Madeline interrupts the traditional routine. The story, told largely in pictures, is colorful and highly amusing.

3. MR. GUMPY'S OUTING

Holt, Rinehart & Winston

John Burningham
Illustrated by the author

Animals and children pile into Mr. Gumpy's boat until it tips over. Summer-fresh colors picture the light-hearted fun. This received the Greenaway Medal, British equivalent of the American Caldecott Medal. The sequel, MR. GUMPY'S MOTOR CAR (Crowell) is equally amusing.

4. MIKE MULLIGAN AND HIS STEAM SHOVEL   Houghton Mifflin
   Virginia Lee Burton
   Illustrated by the author

Mike and his unwanted, outmoded steam shovel, Mary Ann, dig a new and unusual home for themselves in the town of Popperville. A picture story which combines realistic and imaginative elements with humor and appeal.

5. THE VERY HUNGRY CATERPILLAR   Collins
   Eric Carle
   Illustrated by the author

One very little caterpillar abandons his leafy diet for sturdier food and pays for his greed. Bright colors and innovatively cut pages add to this simply presented science and counting book.

6. "CHARLIE NEEDS A CLOAK"   Prentice-Hall
   Tomie De Paola
   Illustrated by the author

Charlie and his favorite sheep introduce the way wool becomes cloth and cloth becomes clothes. Droll illustrations in cheerful colors add a delightful touch of humor.

For slightly older children don't miss the talented author–artist's STREGA NONA (Prentice-Hall), a humorous Italian folktale based on the sorcerer's apprentice theme and THE CLOWN OF GOD (Harcourt, Brace, Jovanovich), the Christmas legend of the Holy Child rendered in joyous, glowing colors against an early Italian renaissance background.

7. THE HAPPY LION   McGraw-Hill
   Louise Fatio
   Illustrated by Roger Duvoisin

So long as the Happy Lion sat peacefully in his little park, everyone in the French village loved him. But when, one day, he went for a stroll through the streets, no one said, "Bonjour Happy Lion"; in fact his best friends fled wildly in every direction, all except one. The happy ending to this sprightly tale is entirely plausible, and the witty, colorful illustrations add to the fun and make the French village as familiar as Main Street.

8. ASK MR. BEAR   Macmillan
   Marjorie Flack
   Illustrated by the author
A little boy did not know what to give his mother for her birthday, but
when he asked Mr. Bear, he received a surprising suggestion that was
just right. Clear-colored pictures add to the charm of this favorite
story of the two- and three-year-olds. Miss Flack's "Angus" books
are equally beloved. ANGUS AND THE DUCKS, ANGUS AND
THE CAT, and ANGUS LOST are published by Doubleday.

9. MILLIONS OF CATS   Coward-McCann
   Wanda Gàg
   Illustrated by the author
The little old man unwisely chose not one, but "millions and billions
and trillions" of cats to keep his lonely wife company at home, with
somewhat startling results. A nonsense tale filled with gay repetitive
rhymes and illustrated with black-and-white drawings.

10. ROSIE'S WALK   Macmillan
    Pat Hutchins
    Illustrated by the author
Rosie the hen takes her walk through the farmyard never aware of the
wicked fox who almost catches her. Illustrations are as humorous and
telling as the brief text.

11. THE SNOWY DAY   Viking
    Ezra Jack Keats
    Illustrated by the author
The solitary play of a three- or four-year-old boy on a snowy day
reflects the experiences any small child might have; only the
illustrations show that he is a Black child. The uncluttered pictures,
part watercolor, part collage, establish the mood and illustrate the
story with rare beauty. *Caldecott Medal,* 1963. WHISTLE FOR
WILLIE, in which a small boy learns to "pucker up" his lips and
whistle for his dog, is another book by this gifted artist. In PETER'S
CHAIR (Harper & Row), Peter reluctantly yields his beloved chair,
now too small, to Susie, his baby sister.

12. MAKE WAY FOR DUCKLINGS   Viking
    Robert McCloskey
    Illustrated by the author

Aided by an Irish policeman, Mr. and Mrs. Mallard and their eight ducklings waddle sedately through the busy traffic of Boston's streets to the Public Gardens, where peanuts and popcorn are plentiful. Perhaps no other author–illustrator for young children has captured so well the flavor of America and the brand of humor that is peculiarly our own. *Caldecott Medal,* 1942. BLUEBERRIES FOR SAL is an equally popular picture tale.

13. THE TALE OF PETER RABBIT   Warne
    Beatrix Potter
    Illustrated by the author
Disobedient Peter loses his fine clothes and almost ends as a rabbit pie when he ventures into Farmer MacGregor's forbidden garden. Distinctive writing and a strong appeal to a small child's sympathies and sense of justice make this an outstanding story. The watercolor illustrations add charm to the narrative by their simplicity of detail and delicacy of color. First published in 1903. BENJAMIN BUNNY, JEMIMA PUDDLE-DUCK, and SQUIRREL NUT-KIN are a few of the author's other titles.

14. WHERE THE WILD THINGS ARE   Harper & Row
    Maurice Sendak
    Illustrated by the author
His wolf costume inspires small Max to such boisterous play that he is ordered to bed. Suddenly the walls of his room disappear, and Max finds himself sailing off to a forest of strange wild creatures who acclaim him their king. Hunger makes Max abandon his royal role, and back he sails, awakening in his own bed and ready for supper. A lyrically told tale of a small rebel and his compensating dream. The illustrations are bizarre and imaginative. *Caldecott Medal,* 1964.

15. WHITE SNOW, BRIGHT SNOW   Lothrop, Lee & Shepard
    Alvin Tresselt
    Illustrated by Roger Duvoisin
The approach of the first snowfall of winter is forecast by the postman, the policeman, the farmer, and the rabbit—all friends of the young child. The description of winter activities and the changes brought about by the coming of spring are told in rhythmic prose that is not only beautiful and vivid but also childlike in its simplicity. *Caldecott*

Medal, 1948. Clear-colored pictures add to the charm of this book, and also to SUN UP, RAIN DROP SPLASH, and HIDE AND SEEK FOG by the same author.

ALPHABET BOOKS

ABC books are very useful for young readers and often prove fascinating to the child in the prereading stage.

16. ANNO'S ALPHABET   Crowell
   Mitsumasa Anno
Imaginatively designed letters fashioned in light wood challenge the viewer's perception of proportions and perspectives. Each letter is framed with a "wit twisting" border. The Japanese artist provides another challenging adventure of the imagination in ANNO'S COUNTING BOOK. These books can be used with older children also.

17. JOHN BURNINGHAM'S ABC   Bobbs-Merrill
   John Burningham
      Illustrated by the author
Bold, colorful illustrations, representing for the most part objects familiar to the younger child, make this a distinctive introductory alphabet book.

18. ABC BUNNY   Coward-McCann
   Wanda Gág
      Illustrated by the author
The rhyming text of this enchanting alphabet has a continuity unusual in ABC books, and there is humor in the unexpected conclusion. One scarlet capital on each page accents the large, dark, superb lithographs. Fortunate the child who learns the alphabet from this book.

19. BRUNO MUNARI'S ABC   Collins
   Bruno Munari
      Illustrated by the author

This artist designs books for children with little text but striking beauty. The large pages make effective use both of clear colors and white space. "F a Fly a Flower a Feather more Flies and a Fish" starts a fly on its way, and it zooms happily through the book to the last page. Such an ABC book has a sensory rather than an ideational appeal and is better, perhaps, for the youngest children but is excellent eyetraining for every age.

20 BRIAN WILDSMITH'S ABC   Watts
    Brian Wildsmith
    Illustrated by the author

One of the most beautiful alphabet books for children, it uses pages in solid colors, rich harmonizing tones of purple, green, rose, and many more, each illustrated with an animal or familiar object and single-word text.

NURSERY AND FOLK TALES

CHICKEN LITTLE (or HENNY PENNY)
GINGERBREAD BOY
LITTLE RED HEN AND THE GRAIN OF WHEAT
THE PANCAKE

Cumulative folk tales which delight small listeners because of the repetition of sound and action.

THE THREE BEARS
THE THREE BILLY GOATS GRUFF √
THE THREE PIGS

Animals tales are early favorites. In the titles listed, repetition pleases the ear, and dramatic action brings a satisfying sense of wonder and surprise. Suggested sources:

21. TOLD UNDER THE GREEN UMBRELLA   Macmillan
    Association for Childhood Education, International, compiler
    Illustrated by Grace Gilkison

22. THE GOLDEN GOOSE BOOK   Warne
   L. Leslie Brooke
   Illustrated by the author

23. CHIMNEY CORNER STORIES   Putnam
   Veronica Hutchinson, compiler
   Illustrated by Lois Lenski

24. THE THREE BEARS AND FIFTEEN OTHER STORIES   Crowell
   Anne Rockwell, selector
   Illustrated by the selector

25. THE SHOEMAKER AND THE ELVES   Scribner's
   Jakob and Wilhelm Grimm
   Illustrated by Adrienne Adams
   This favorite folk tale is given new dimension with Adrienne Adams'
   appealing pictures.

26. ONE FINE DAY   Macmillan
   Nonny Hogrogian
   Illustrated by the author
   His thieving ways cost a greedy fox his tail, and he needed the help of
   many friends before he could regain it! Preschoolers will enjoy the
   cumulative story illustrated with strong, expressive pictures. *Caldecott Medal, 1972.*

27. ANANSI, THE SPIDER   Holt, Rinehart & Winston
   Gerald McDermott, adapter
   Illustrated by the adapter
   Adapted from an animated film of the same title, this is a highly
   effective picture book presentation of how Anansi, West African folk
   hero, falls into trouble, is rescued by his six sons, and then has
   difficulty deciding which one deserves the prize. Stunning in design
   and color.

RHYMES AND POETRY

28. FROG WENT A-COURTIN'　　　　　Harcourt Brace Jovanovich
    John Langstaff, editor
    Illustrated by Feodor Rojankovsky
Choice animal illustrations rich in colorful detail add to the charm of
this version of the long popular ballad of Frog's wooing of little Miss
Mousie. *Caldecott Medal*, 1956.

29. IN A SPRING GARDEN　　　　　　　　　　　　　　　Dial
    Richard Lewis, editor
    Illustrated by Ezra Jack Keats
　　　　　　　　　　Just simply alive,
　　　　　　　　　　Both of us, I
　　　　　　　　　　And the poppy.
　　　　　　　　　　　　—Issa
These brief lines exemplify the spirit of this fine introductory
collection of twenty-eight haiku which follow a day in spring from a
red morning sky to the passing of a giant firefly. The vivid collage and
watercolor illustrations perfectly complement the verses.

30. THE NIGHT BEFORE CHRISTMAS　　　　Grosset & Dunlap
    Clement C. Moore
    Illustrated by Leonard Weisgard
Christmas would be incomplete without this American classic. Santa,
with his "sleigh full of toys and eight tiny reindeer," sailing through
wintry skies, mounting to the housetops, popping down chimneys to
fill waiting stockings—this Santa has become our national symbol of
Christmas gaiety and giving. Children learn this long narrative poem
with a few hearings and love it always. Originally published in 1823.
Another attractive edition is THE NIGHT BEFORE CHRIST-
MAS, illustrated by Arthur Rackham (Lippincott).

31. THE REAL MOTHER GOOSE　　　　　　　Rand McNally
    Illustrated by Blanche Fisher Wright
In 1965 the publishers issued a Fiftieth Anniversary Edition of this
popular old book, with an introduction by Mrs. Arbuthnot concerning

the history of the Mother Goose verses. Pictures are large, clear, and colorful, and there are over four hundred verses. It is a particularly useful edition with the youngest children. Other editions are: BOOK OF NURSERY AND MOTHER GOOSE RHYMES, illustrated by Marguerite De Angeli (Doubleday), THE MOTHER GOOSE BOOK, illustrated by Alice and Martin Provensen (Random), THE MOTHER GOOSE TREASURY, illustrated by Raymond Briggs (Coward–McCann), and RING O' ROSES, illustrated by L. Leslie Brooke (Warne).

32. SING-SONG   Macmillan
    Christina Rossetti
    Illustrated by Marguerite Davis
Simple rhythmic verses about frisky lambs and merry children, the wind that "never rests," the caterpillar "brown and furry," and "timid, funny, brisk little bunny," who "winks his nose and sits all sunny." Unsurpassed in lyric quality and childlike spontaneity, these verses, originally published in 1872, are excellent to use following Mother Goose.

33. THE FOX WENT OUT ON A CHILLY NIGHT   Doubleday
    Illustrated by Peter Spier
The old folk song about the escapades of a hungry fox is introduced in handsome picture-book format, with illustrations rich in color and detail. Music is appended so that the short rhythmic verses can be sung or read.

34. A CHILD'S GARDEN OF VERSES   Grosset & Dunlap
    Robert Louis Stevenson
    Illustrated by Gyo Fujikawa
Stevenson once said, "I am one of the few people in the world who do not forget their own lives." Because of the power he has of identifying himself with the child, his poems are beloved by English-speaking children everywhere. Originally published in England under the title PENNY WHISTLES in 1885. Another attractive edition is: A CHILD'S GARDEN OF VERSES, illustrated by Erik Blegvad (Random).

35. MOMMY, BUY ME A CHINA DOLL   Farrar, Straus & Giroux
    Harve Zemach
    Illustrated by Margot Zemach

When Eliza Lou begs for a china doll, her mother ponders aloud how they can manage to buy it. Children soon participate in the responses in this repetitive children's song from the Ozarks, illustrated with distinction.

BIBLE STORIES

36. THE CHRIST CHILD   Doubleday
    Illustrated by Maud and Miska Petersham

In this picture book, which tells the story of the Nativity, it is indeed fortunate that the Petershams have used the biblical text with its poetic beauty and simple dignity. The illustrations interpret the spirit of the Holy Land with reverence, and their glowing colors delight the eye.

37. NOAH'S ARK   Doubleday
    Illustrated by Peter Spier

Preceded by Peter Spier's own translation of a 17th century Dutch poem about the Deluge, dramatic scenes of the ark afloat on the great waters contrast with humorous interior ones of Noah and his menagerie. The lovely translucent colors and many details create a delightful interpretation of this Old Testament story.

For Children 6, 7, and 8

PICTURE BOOKS AND STORIES

38. THE DESERT IS THEIRS   Scribner's
    Byrd Baylor
    Illustrated by Peter Parnell

Lyrical prose and carefully done pen and ink drawings tell of the closeness of the Papago Indians to the land and its creatures. Another fine book by this author–artist team is HAWK, I'M YOUR BROTHER, which describes the relationship between an Indian boy of the Southwest and a captured hawk.

39. THE LITTLE HOUSE   Houghton Mifflin
    Virginia Lee Burton
    Illustrated by the author

The little house was very happy as she sat on the quiet hillside watching the changing seasons. As the years passed, however, tall buildings grew up around her, and the noise of the city traffic disturbed her. She became sad and lonely until one day someone who understood her need for twinkling stars overhead and dancing apple blossoms moved her back to just the right little hill. The rhythmic quality of the text is beautifully reproduced in the illustrations. *Caldecott Medal, 1943.*

40. DID YOU CARRY THE FLAG TODAY, CHARLEY?
                                        Holt, Rinehart & Winston
    Rebecca Caudill
    Illustrated by Nancy Grossman

This is the question his parents, brothers, and sisters ask Charley each day when the bus returns him from a summer school for four- and five-

13

year-olds. Unfortunately Charley's curiosity always gets him into trouble, and it is a long time before he wins the coveted honor. An engagingly told story of a very real little boy who lives in the Appalachian mountain country. Equally appealing is the author's A POCKETFUL OF CRICKET, with the same regional background, illustrated by Evaline Ness.

41. HENRY HUGGINS   Morrow
    Beverly Cleary
    Illustrated by Louis Darling
A lively, humorous tale about Henry, a third-grader, and his dog, Ribsy, who is his companion on many an escapade. The author's understanding of small boys, their interests and activities, lends weight to a book whose popularity, since it was first published in 1950, is equalled by the many sequels which have followed it. The author has also written several wise and witty stories about another engaging character, strong-willed Ramona.

42. THE COURAGE OF SARAH NOBLE   Scribner's
    Alice Dalgliesh
    Illustrated by Leonard Weisgard
When her mother wrapped Sarah Noble in a warm new cloak, she said, "Keep up your courage, Sarah Noble." And eight-year-old Sarah had need of this advice, for she was journeying on foot into the wilderness with her father to cook and care for him. When unfriendly settlers scowled at her, or wolves howled near them in the forest, or Indians came near, Sarah hugged her cloak around her, remembered her mother's words, and managed to survive. Based on a true episode, this story of a child's fortitude is movingly told.

43. THE 500 HATS OF BARTHOLOMEW CUBBINS   Vanguard
    Theodor Seuss Geisel (pseud. Dr. Seuss)
    Illustrated by the author
One of the funniest tales of the last four decades! Bartholomew's hat troubles never lose their charm. As gravely told as a folk tale, the story's humor grows with each reading. There is grim suspense and a conclusion that satisfies everyone, including Bartholomew. Its sequel, BARTHOLOMEW AND THE OOBLECK (Random), is equally popular. Favorites with children under six are AND TO THINK THAT I SAW IT ON MULBERRY STREET (Vanguard) and the

rhyming nonsense of HORTON HATCHES THE EGG (Random).

44. NEW ILLUSTRATED JUST-SO STORIES   Doubleday
    Rudyard Kipling
    Illustrated by Nicolas
Older children can read Kipling's JUST-SO STORIES for themselves, but this edition is particularly satisfying to young children
because of its colorful picture-book format. When they hear the
stories read aloud, they chuckle over the funny words and the
sonorous sentences. JUST-SO STORIES was originally published
in 1902.

45. THE STORY OF FERDINAND   Viking
    Munro Leaf
    Illustrated by Robert Lawson
What happens when a gentle bull who loves to smell flowers is goaded
into temporary fierceness by the sting of a bee! Ferdinand's incon-
gruous affection for flowers captured the public fancy four decades
ago, and the children have loyally retained him as a favorite picture-
book character.

46. FROG AND TOAD TOGETHER   Harper & Row
    Arnold Lobel
    Illustrated by the author
A collection of five delightfully humorous stories about two best
friends, with perfect illustrations in soft greens and browns. A fine
example of I-Can-Read Books.

47. WINNIE-THE-POOH   Dutton
    Alan A. Milne
    Illustrated by Ernest Shepard
Six-year-old Christopher Robin listens to stories about his toy pets,
Rabbit, Piglet, Eeyore the Donkey, Kanga and Baby Roo, and
especially about Winnie-the-Pooh, the Bear of Little Brain, one of the
most captivating characters in children's literature. The magic of Mr.
Milne's prose endows these playthings with distinct individuality,
aided by Ernest Shepard's drawings, which are an integral part of the
book. This is a prime favorite for reading aloud to the entire family.
Followed by HOUSE AT POOH CORNER. THE WORLD OF
POOH offers both these titles in a single, color-illustrated volume.

48. LITTLE BEAR

Else Minarik

Illustrated by Maurice Sendak

Harper & Row

This book and its successors—FATHER BEAR COMES HOME, KISS FOR LITTLE BEAR, LITTLE BEAR'S FRIENDS, LITTLE BEAR'S VISIT—are among the best of easy-to-read publications. Little Bear and his mother are prototypes of any little boy and his loving mama. The stories center on Little Bear's play, but always the theme of Mother's understanding and love comes through with enough humor to prevent over-sweetness. Maurice Sendak's illustrations make the antics and charm of Little Bear irresistible.

49. THE BIGGEST BEAR

Lynd Ward

Illustrated by the author

Houghton Mifflin

Johnny Orchard never did acquire the bearskin for which he boldly went hunting. Instead, he brought home a cuddly bear cub, which grew in size and appetite to mammoth proportions and worried his family and neighbors half to death! An ingenuous and happy solution ends this highly humorous tale, which is superbly illustrated and ageless in appeal. *Caldecott Medal,* 1953.

50. CROW BOY

Taro Yashima

Illustrated by the author

Viking

Chibi, shy, lonely and afraid, walks daily to the village school from his Japanese farm home. An understanding teacher discovers his remarkable skill in imitating the sounds of the crows and helps make the class aware of it, too. On graduation day, Chibi is honored for his perfect attendance, and, best of all, his schoolmates greet him with the nickname Crow Boy in honor of his special talent. This sensitive story, which reflects the experiences of many lonely children, is illustrated with colorful crayon drawings.

FOLK AND FAIRY TALES AND FABLES

These are tales of magic and enchantment, of kindly dwarfs and wicked witches, hard-pressed lassies and talking beasts, and there is one tall-tale hound dog that is pure Americana. Each generation enjoys hearing these old tales, and there is added pleasure in the modern illustrated editions.

SINGLE TALES IN PICTURE BOOK FORM

51. WHY MOSQUITOS BUZZ IN PEOPLE'S EARS: A
    WEST AFRICAN FOLKTALE   Dial
    Verna Aardema
    Illustrated by Leo and Diane Dillon
    Caldecott Medal, 1976

Hans Christian Andersen: 52–55

52. THE NIGHTINGALE   Harper & Row
    Illustrated by Nancy Burkert

53. THE STEADFAST TIN SOLDIER   Scribner's
    Illustrated by Marcia Brown

54. THE UGLY DUCKLING   Scribner's
    Illustrated by Adrienne Adams

55. THE WILD SWANS   Scribner's
    Illustrated by Marcia Brown

56. THE FAST SOONER HOUND   Houghton Mifflin
    Arna Bontemps and Jack Conroy
    Illustrated by Virginia Lee Burton

57. ONCE A MOUSE   Scribner's
    Illustrated by Marcia Brown
    Caldecott Medal, 1962

58. CHANTICLEER AND THE FOX   Crowell
    Geoffrey Chaucer
    Illustrated by Barbara Cooney
    Caldecott Medal, 1959

Jakob and Wilhelm Grimm: 59–62

59. HANSEL AND GRETEL   Delacorte
    Illustrated by Arnold Lobel

60. RAPUNZEL   Harcourt Brace Jovanovich
Illustrated by Felix Hoffmann

61. SNOW WHITE AND ROSE RED   Scribner's
Illustrated by Adrienne Adams

62. SNOW WHITE AND THE SEVEN DWARFS
                          Coward, McCann & Geohegan
Illustrated by Wanda Gág

63. THE WAVE   Houghton Mifflin
Margaret Hodges, adapter
Illustrated by Blair Lent

64. DICK WHITTINGTON AND HIS CAT   Scribner's
Joseph Jacobs
Illustrated by Marcia Brown

65. JOHN HENRY: AN AMERICAN LEGEND   Pantheon
Illustrated by Ezra Jack Keats

66. THE FUNNY LITTLE WOMAN   Dutton
Arlene Mosel
Illustrated by Blair Lent
Caldecott Medal, 1973

Charles Perrault: 67, 68

67. CINDERELLA   Scribner's
Illustrated by Marcia Brown
Caldecott Medal, 1955

68. PUSS IN BOOTS   Scribner's
Illustrated by Marcia Brown

69. THE FOOL OF THE WORLD AND THE FLYING SHIP
                            Farrar, Straus & Giroux
Arthur Ransome, reteller
Illustrated by Uri Shulevitz
Caldecott Medal, 1969

70. THE MAGIC COOKING POT: A FOLKTALE OF INDIA
                               Houghton Mifflin
Faith M. Towle, reteller and illustrator

71. DUFFY AND THE DEVIL: A CORNISH FOLKTALE

Farrar, Straus & Giroux

Harve Zemach, reteller
Illustrated by Margot Zemach
Caldecott Medal, 1974

COLLECTIONS OF FOLK TALES AND FABLES

72. AESOP'S FABLES   Grosset & Dunlap
Illustrated by Fritz Kredel

73. FABLES OF AESOP   Macmillan
Joseph Jacobs, editor
Illustrated by David Levine

These short allegorical stories in which animals are given human characteristics in order to point out a moral are part of the world's lasting literature. The use of individual fables with children is to be recommended, for they are childlike in their emphasis on the simpler virtues and in the impersonal quality of their telling.

74. EAST OF THE SUN AND WEST OF THE MOON,
    AND OTHER TALES   Macmillan
Peter Asbjørnsen and Jørgen Moe
Illustrated by Tom Vroman

Jakob and Wilhelm Grimm: 75, 76

FAIRY TALES

The brothers Grimm were thirteen years collecting these tales in rural Germany. To them, children are indebted for the well-loved HANSEL AND GRETEL, SNOW WHITE AND THE SEVEN DWARFS, RUMPELSTILTSKIN, THE BRAVE LITTLE TAILOR, and many others. There are numerous editions of these stories, and the following are to be recommended:

75. GRIMM'S FAIRY TALES   Grosset & Dunlap
Illustrated by Fritz Kredel

76. TALES FROM GRIMM   Coward, McCann & Geoghegan
Freely translated and illustrated by Wanda Gág

77. THE FAIRY TALE TREASURY   Coward, McCann & Geoghegan
    Virginia Haviland, compiler
    Illustrated by Raymond Briggs

78. THE PROVENSEN BOOK OF FAIRY TALES   Random
    Alice and Martin Provensen, compilers
    Illustrated by the Provensens

79. ARTHUR RACKHAM FAIRY BOOK   Lippincott
    Illustrated by Arthur Rackham

RHYMES AND POETRY

80. TIME FOR POETRY (3rd General Edition)   Scott, Foresman
    May Hill Arbuthnot and Shelton L. Root, Jr., editors
    Illustrated by Arthur Paul
A fine anthology, unusual in its selection of almost eight hundred poems to be read to boys and girls four to fourteen. Poems are on subjects which appeal to children, and there is a special group, "Wisdom and Beauty," "to help young spirits soar." Selections range from the old nursery rhymes to outstanding modern poets and are distinctive for their melody, movement, and imaginative quality. There is a helpful introduction for adults on the enjoyment of poetry with children.

81. THE LITTLE HILL   Harcourt Brace Jovanovich
    Harry Behn
    Illustrated by the author
The poems in this small book range from lighthearted nonsense verse for the youngest to authentic lyric poetry for the oldest children. Beautiful in format and content, this is a fresh and important contribution to poetry for children.

82. UNDER THE TENT OF THE SKY   Macmillan
    John E. Brewton, compiler
    Illustrated by Robert Lawson
A companion to Sara and John Brewton's GAILY WE PARADE,

this anthology of poetry about animals is a choice one. With wild and domestic animals, insects, fish, birds, and "wee beasties" of every variety, these poems, both serious and humorous in mood, delight young children. Robert Lawson's illustrations add vitality and beauty to the verses.

83. THE BIRDS AND THE BEASTS WERE THERE   Collins
    William Cole, editor
    Illustrated by Helen Siegl

This splendid collection of poems about all sorts of animals contains some nonsense verses but there is also much about man's cruelty to animals. Chiefly though these poems sing of the beauty and grace of animals and the "honesty of their instincts," for this anthology is as sound biologically as it is poetically. For somewhat older children don't miss Mr. Cole's OH, WHAT NONSENSE! (Viking) which offers fifty "rib-tickling" poems illustrated with Tomi Ungerer's black-and-white sketches and PICK ME UP: A BOOK OF SHORT SHORT POEMS (Macmillan).

84. COMPLETE NONSENSE BOOK   Dodd, Mead
    Edward Lear
    Illustrated by the author

"The Owl and the Pussy Cat," "The Pobble Who Had No Toes," "The Jumblies," and hundreds of other daft and delightful verses by Edward Lear have made nonsense verses popular both with children and adults since he began to write them in 1846. Lear's amusing illustrations make his NONSENSE BOOKS as much fun to look at as to read and listen to.

85. WHEN WE WERE VERY YOUNG   Dutton
    NOW WE ARE SIX
    Alan A. Milne
    Illustrated by Ernest Shepard

Perhaps the best light verse ever written for young children, these two books are full of nonsense, whimsy, and unexpected imaginings, but no fairies. The everyday world of the child comes gaily alive and is served up in dancing rhythms, with absurd words and jokes to add to the fun. Skillful line drawings by Ernest Shepard are a perfect accompaniment. A special edition with added color plates, THE

86. HAILSTONES AND HALIBUT BONES   Doubleday
    Mary O'Neill
    Illustrated by Leonard Weisgard
Distinctive rhythmic verses describe a dozen different colors and
explore in many dimensions the part each color plays in the world of
nature, play, and imagination. Leonard Weisgard has illustrated each
of the poems in tones of its own particular color in this stimulating and
highly original small volume.

87. ALL THE SILVER PENNIES   Macmillan
    Blanche Jennings Thompson, editor
    Decorations by Ursula Arndt
Within a handsome single volume are SILVER PENNIES, a favorite
anthology of familiar poetry for over forty years, and MORE
SILVER PENNIES. Prefatory remarks give a feel for the theme or
spirit of each poem.

BIBLE STORIES AND PRAYERS

88. DAVID   Macmillan
    JOSEPH AND HIS BROTHERS
These stories of Bible heroes have special appeal for children because
of the dramatic movement of events. Maud and Miska Petersham
have illustrated the above editions of the separate stories.

89. THE BOOK OF PSALMS, OLD TESTAMENT
    Twenty-third Psalm
There is a reassuring, comforting quality about the Psalms which
children need. The Twenty-third Psalm, with its message of God's
care for his children, is usually the best introduction to this great body
of literature.

90. JONAH: AN OLD TESTAMENT STORY   Lippincott
    Beverly Brodsky, reteller and illustrator
Jonah's struggles with the leviathan and with himself are brought out
through the elemental force of the artist's glowing paintings.

9 t. BLESS THIS DAY   Harcourt Brace Jovanovich
  Elfrida Vipont
  Illustrated by Harold Jones

This book of devotions may be used by the whole family. There are little graces for the youngest, some of the matchless collects for growing children and adults, and selections from ancient breviaries, that everyone should know. The prayers are grouped for waking, for others, for guidance, for thanksgiving and praise, and for benediction, to mention a few. The illustrations by Harold Jones both in black and white and color are as full of grace as the prayers and add to the beauty of this choice book.

BIOGRAPHY

92. THE COLUMBUS STORY   Scribner's
  Alice Dalgliesh
  Illustrated by Leo Politi

Leo Politi's numerous illustrations in glowing colors make this a handsome introductory picture biography for younger readers.

93. BENJAMIN FRANKLIN   Doubleday
  Edgar and Igri d'Aulaire
  Illustrated by the authors

Full of homely details and wisely selected anecdotes, this picture-story biography serves as a convincing and appreciative introduction to a man who played an important role in our country's history. Maxims from the famous POOR RICHARD'S ALMANAC appear in marginal decorations on many pages.

94. WILL YOU SIGN HERE, JOHN HANCOCK?
                                        Coward, McCann & Geoghegan
  Jean Fritz
  Illustrated by Trina Schart Hyman

One of John Hancock's most noticeable characteristics was his vanity. That quality, along with his charm and ambition, are highlighted in this lighthearted look at one of our Founding Fathers whose signature is so prominent on the Declaration of Independence. Another of Miss Fritz's lively biographies of American Revolutionary figures is WHERE WAS PATRICK HENRY ON THE 29th OF MAY? illustrated by Margot Tomes.

For Children 9, 10, and 11

FICTION

95. MR. POPPER'S PENGUINS   Little, Brown
    Richard and Florence Atwater
    Illustrated by Robert Lawson

Life in the Popper family was never quite the same after Mr. Popper received a penguin as a gift from an Antarctic explorer. This genuinely funny modern nonsense tale has readily won a place for itself among young readers. Excellent for reading aloud.

96. THE CHILDREN OF GREEN KNOWE
                                    Harcourt Brace Jovanovich
    Lucy M. Boston
    Illustrated by Peter Boston

When Tolly comes to Green Knowe to vacation with his great-grandmother, he finds the children who lived there in the seventeenth century. Sometimes he only hears them or sees them in a mirror, but sometimes he actually talks with them. So skillfully does the author move from one century to another that the past mingles with the present in the old castle where many generations have lived. Beautifully written and first published in England, this is a story for the imaginative child. Another distinguished story with the background of Green Knowe is a modern realistic animal story, A STRANGER AT GREEN KNOWE.

97. CADDIE WOODLAWN   Macmillan
    Carol R. Brink
    Illustrated by Trina Schart Hyman

Life on the Wisconsin frontier in the 1860s becomes very real and vivid in this story of tomboy Caddie and her two brothers. Noted for its fine characterization and good background. *Newbery Medal,* 1936.

98. THE FAMILY UNDER THE BRIDGE   Harper & Row
    Natalie Savage Carlson
    Illustrated by Garth Williams
Armand, a lovable old Paris hobo, lived a free, irresponsible life until three homeless children moved into his shelter under the bridge, and into his heart as well. He clings to his freedom as long as possible, but becomes a workingman for the sake of his "starlings" and makes their wish come true. A heartwarming story told with lightness and humor, it brings the flavors and scenes of the Paris which Armand loved. The author's HAPPY ORPHELINE and A BROTHER FOR THE ORPHELINES are two other tales delightfully French in flavor.

99. ROBINSON CRUSOE   Macmillan
    Daniel Defoe
    Illustrated by Federico Castellon
Being shipwrecked and cast ashore on a desert island is a fate most boys envy, and each generation admires the ingenuity and bravery of Robinson Crusoe in his struggle for existence. Although Defoe wrote this story in 1719 for adult readers, children through the years have claimed it for their own. Another recommended edition is: ROBIN-SON CRUSOE, illustrated by Lynd Ward (Grosset & Dunlap).

100. THE WHEEL ON THE SCHOOL   Harper & Row
    Meindert De Jong
    Illustrated by Maurice Sendak
It was Lina, the only girl in the school, who wondered why there were no storks on the roofs of Shora, a small Dutch fishing village. Under the wise direction of the schoolmaster, plus the united efforts of the entire community, a wheel is found, and a pair of storks rescued from the storm-tossed sea set up housekeeping on the roof of the school. This author goes deeply into the heart of childhood and has written a moving story, filled with suspense and distinguished for the quality of its writing. *Newbery Medal,* 1955.

101. ALICE'S ADVENTURES IN WONDERLAND   Macmillan
    THROUGH THE LOOKING GLASS
    Charles Lutwidge Dodgson (pseud. Lewis Carroll)
    Illustrated by John Tenniel

A highly imaginative master mathematician tells two stories of a little girl's dream journeys into lands of enchantment. Children share Alice's wonder as one magical event follows another, while grownups find keen enjoyment in the author's philosophy and humor. The Mad Hatter, Tweedledum and Tweedledee, the Dormouse, the White Rabbit, the Red and White Queens, the Cheshire Cat, and other characters have all won permanent places in the child's book world. First published in 1865. Another recommended edition is: ALICE IN WONDERLAND AND THROUGH THE LOOKING GLASS, illustrated by John Tenniel (Grosset & Dunlap).

✓ 102. THE MATCHLOCK GUN   Dodd, Mead
   Walter Edmonds
   Illustrated by Paul Lantz
In his father's absence young Edward fires an heirloom gun and saves his family from an Indian attack. A well-known writer of historical fiction has based this dramatic story on a true incident of the French and Indian Wars. *Newbery Medal,* 1942.

103. THE MIDDLE MOFFAT   Harcourt Brace Jovanovich
   Eleanor Estes
   Illustrated by Louis Slobodkin
Janey was a serious little girl to whom surprising things always happened. Her mishaps performing in a play and at an organ recital are among the most sparkling chapters in this book. A humorous yet sensitively told story which shows true insight into the feelings of a medium-sized little girl and surrounds her with a real and convincing family atmosphere. Two other entertaining books in this series are THE MOFFATS and RUFUS M.

104. THE GREAT BRAIN (and other titles)   Dial
   John D. Fitzgerald
   Illustrated by Mercer Mayer
The author and the artist have successfully combined their talents to produce a series of delightful stories about a Roman Catholic family who lived in a Mormon town during the late 1800s. The lively doings center on Tom Fitzgerald, the Great Brain, who is a master at devising schemes and is glib of tongue.

105. BLUE WILLOW   Viking
    Doris Gates
    Illustrated by Paul Lantz
Janey Larkin longed for the day when her family could once again
enjoy real home life instead of their roving existence as cotton pickers
in the San Joaquin Valley of California. A thought-provoking novel,
rich in social values and family and community life.

106. WIND IN THE WILLOWS   Scribner's
    Kenneth Grahame
    Illustrated by Ernest Shepard
Magic, beauty, and friendly humor are found in these unforgettable
stories of small animal adventures first told by the author to his little
son. Written with rare artistry, the book is a perfect reading-aloud
choice for all ages. Ernest Shepard's pen-and-ink drawings capture
the spirit of the text. In the revised edition eight new full color pictures
have been added.

107. KING OF THE WIND   Rand McNally
    Marguerite Henry
    Illustrated by Wesley Dennis
This is the moving story of the Godolphin Arabian that put his stamp
on racehorse thoroughbreds, including our own Man o' War. In every
one of her well-written animal stories, Mrs. Henry also creates
unforgettable human characters. The little mute boy who guarded
King of the Wind is a memorable example. *Newbery Medal,* 1949.
Pictures by Wesley Dennis add appeal to this book and to the ever-
popular JUSTIN MORGAN HAD A HORSE, MISTY OF
CHINCOTEAGUE, and BRIGHTY OF THE GRAND CAN-
YON.

108. THE MOUSE AND HIS CHILD   Harper & Row
    Russell Hoban
    Illustrated by Lillian Hoban
A wind-up tin toy—a mouse and his child—discarded on a rubbish
heap where Manny Rat is a threat is found and repaired by a tramp.
The toy pair set out on a long journey in seach of a home and family.
There are humor and tenderness, cruelty and violence in this complex
fantasy which will convey varying depths of meaning to different age
groups.

109. THE JUNGLE BOOK   Grosset & Dunlap
   Rudyard Kipling
   Illustrated by Fritz Eichenberg
Stories of the East Indian jungles and of Mowgli, who, although human, was adopted by the wolf pack and taught the laws of the jungle by Bagheers the panther and Baloo the bear. Other favorite tales in this volume are "Rikki-Tikki-Tavi" and the "Toomai of the Elephants." First published in 1894. Another edition is: THE JUNGLE BOOK, illustrated by Robert Shore (Macmillan).

110. FROM THE MIXED-UP FILES OF
   MRS. BASIL E. FRANKWEILER   Atheneum
   E. L. Konigsburg
   Illustrated by the author
Two modern, resourceful children—eleven-year-old Claudia and her nine-year-old brother—are featured in this engaging story of their runaway adventures in the Metropolitan Museum of Art where they become involved with an eccentric old lady and a mysterious statue. *Newbery Medal,* 1968. In the same year the author's JENNIFER, HECATE, MACBETH, WILLIAM MCKINLEY, AND ME, ELIZABETH, the story of an interracial friendship, was voted a Newbery Honor Book.

111. RABBIT HILL   Viking
   Robert Lawson
   Illustrated by the author
Here is an animal fantasy of a high order. Father Rabbit, a Southern gentleman of the old school, Mother Rabbit, the worrying kind, their son Georgie, and crusty old Uncle Analdas share in the excitement of the small creatures of Rabbit Hill when they learn that "New Folks" are coming to live in the Big House. "I do hope they're planting Folks," says Mother Rabbit, and so they prove to be, for they plant an extra large garden with plenty for all. The author has created a fresh, lively, and amusing world and has made drawings that are unusual in their careful execution and in their beauty. *Newbery Medal,* 1945. A sequel is TOUGH WINTER.

112. STRAWBERRY GIRL   Lippincott
   Lois Lenski
   Illustrtaed by the author

Young Birdie Boyer eagerly joins in to help her family work their small, newly acquired Florida backwoods farm. In addition, she starts a modest reform in Shoestring Slater and his shiftless, pesky family nearby! An authentic regional tale told with humor and vigor. *Newbery Medal,* 1946.

113. THE LION, THE WITCH AND THE WARDROBE   Macmillan
    C. S. Lewis
    Illustrated by Pauline Baynes
The distinguished author of THE SCREWTAPE LETTERS wrote this children's story for his godchild, and so began the NARNIA stories, outstanding modern fairy tales with an underlying theme of good overcoming evil. In this first title, four English children walk through the wardrobe in a strange home they are visiting and enter the cold, wintry land of Narnia, which is suffering under the spell of the White Witch. They are guided to the noble lion Aslan and loyally aid him in freeing Narnia and its inhabitants from their unhappy fate.

114. ADVENTURES OF PINOCCHIO   Macmillan
    Carlo Lorenzini (pseud. C. Collodi)
    Illustrated by Attilio Mussino
The story of a mischievous, saucy little marionette who finally became a real boy is just as beloved today as when it appeared in Italy almost a hundred years ago. Another suggested edition is: ADVEN-TURES OF PINOCCHIO, illustrated by Fritz Kredel (Grosset & Dunlap).

115. HOMER PRICE   Viking
    Robert McCloskey
    Illustrated by the author
Where Route 56 meets 56A in the small midwestern town of Centerburg, Homer Price catches burglars with his pet skunk, copes with a ferocious doughnut machine in his uncle's lunchroom, and exposes the supercolossal comic strip hero, Super Duper. Text and pictures are pure Americana, hilarious and convincing in their portrayal of midwestern small-town life.

116. THE BORROWERS   Harcourt Brace Jovanovich
    Mary Norton
    Illustrated by Beth and Joe Krush

Fascinating fantasy about a tiny family that lived beneath the kitchen floor of an old English country house and "borrowed" from the larger human residents to fill their modest needs. Their sudden discovery by a small boy visitor almost proves to be their undoing. The imaginative details about the activities of the miniature people have tremendous appeal for children. Illustrations by Beth and Joe Krush are a perfect complement to this title and three others in the series: THE BOR-ROWERS AFIELD, THE BORROWERS AFLOAT, and THE BORROWERS ALOFT.

117. TOM'S MIDNIGHT GARDEN   Lippincott
    A. Philippa Pearce
    Illustrated by Susan Einzig

One night when the grandfather clock strikes thirteen, Tom, going downstairs to investigate, finds a marvelous garden where nightly thereafter he has wonderful adventures with Hetty, a girl of the late Victorian era. Published in 1958 and awarded the Carnegie Medal as the outstanding English children's book of the year, this is one of the best time fantasies ever written for young readers.

118. OTTO OF THE SILVER HAND   Scribner's
    Howard Pyle
    Illustrated by the author

The story of Otto, the son of a German robber baron, and his adventures in a time of cruel war and deadly feuds. Howard Pyle has done some of his best work in this story of a gentle boy who held to his own ideas of right although they were opposed to the spirit of the age. First published in 1888.

119. HENRY REED, INC.   Viking
    Keith Robertson
    Illustrated by Robert McCloskey

In a genuinely funny modern tale, young Henry Reed, aided by twelve-year-old Midge Glass, launches into a free enterprise project to earn money during a summer holiday. With "research" activities ranging from earthworms to balloons, Henry and Midge achieve a highly profitable and well-publicized school holiday. Robert McClos-key's illustrations are as unforgettably and typically Americana as in his earlier HOMER PRICE. There are several sequels.

𝒪 120. VERONICA GANZ   Doubleday
   Marilyn Sachs
   Illustrated by Louis Glanzman
Overgrown Veronica, skilled in the use of fist and tongue, is the
scourge of the eighth-grade class. Not until undersized Peter comes on
the scene, outwitting and enraging her by his shrewd anticipation of
her every move, and then admitting his admiration for her, does
Veronica discover that it is more satisfying to be admired than to be
feared. In a sequel, PETER AND VERONICA, the author deals
perceptively and honestly with the matter of prejudice.

121 BAMBI   Grosset & Dunlap
   Felix Salten
   Illustrated by Kurt Wiese
Bambi is a deer of the Danube forest whose story is told from the time
he is a newly-born fawn until he becomes an antlered stag. The
narrative is poetic, sympathetic, and filled with the forest sights and
sounds which are part of Bambi's experience. Another edition is:
BAMBI: A LIFE IN THE WOODS, illustrated by Barbara Cooney
(Simon & Schuster).

122. THE GOOD MASTER   Viking
   Kate Seredy
   Illustrated by the author
Motherless Kate was an irrepressible little hoyden until she was
brought to her uncle's ranch and placed under his steadying influence
and that of her cousin Jansci. The story of early twentieth-century
Hungary is told with zest and humor by its Hungarian-born author-
artist.

123. CALL IT COURAGE   Macmillan
   Armstrong Sperry
   Illustrated by the author
Mafatu overcomes his fear of the sea in a heroic gesture which wins
back for him the respect of his fellow tribesmen of a South Sea island.
The author's fine illustrations, dramatic narrative, and constructive
theme, make this a distinguished story. *Newbery Medal,* 1941.

124. HEIDI   Grosset & Dunlap
   Johanna Spyri
   Illustrated by William Sharp

An old and well-loved story of the Swiss mountain girl Heidi, whose joyous nature wins the affection of her gruff old grandfather and all who know her. The simple story of her life in the mountain hut amidst the beauty of snow-capped Alps has had a great deal of appeal for children since it appeared in 1880. This translation by Helen B. Dole is considered the best.

125. WINTER DANGER   Harcourt Brace Jovanovich
  William Steele
  Illustrated by Paul Galdone

Caje and his father are completely at odds. The father knows only of the rough dangers of the hunter's life; Caje yearns for security and the ordered life of the settler-farmers. The boy gets his wish, but discovers that the only security in this world must be won the hard way by one's own efforts. This is only one example of William Steele's ability to make pioneer days vividly alive for modern children. In WILDER-NESS JOURNEY, FAR FRONTIER, and other books, he shows stout-hearted boys blundering, learning, and growing in an adventurous struggle for survival.

126. ABEL'S ISLAND   Farrar, Straus & Giroux
  William Steig
  Illustrated by the author

A rich and pampered mouse named Abelard Hassam de Chirico Flint is swept from the side of his beloved bride during a storm and eventually is marooned on an uninhabited island where he must call upon brain and brawn power he never knew he had in order to survive. The literary style is pure joy! The story is enthralling! Wonderful for family sharing. This author-artist has also done some delightful picture stories for younger readers.

127. HONK: THE MOOSE   Dodd, Mead
  Phil Stong
  Illustrated by Kurt Wiese

When hungry Honk found shelter from the cold in a livery stable, not even the town policeman could budge him from his snug retreat. A cheerful winter's tale of an enterprising moose and the excitement he created in a peaceful Minnesota town.

128. MARY POPPINS   Harcourt Brace Jovanovich
  Pamela Travers
  Illustrated by Mary Shepard

From the time that Mary Poppins, the new nursemaid, slid gracefully up the bannister, until, holding fast to her parrot-handled umbrella, she was carried away by the West Wind, the Banks children never knew a dull moment. This fantastic nonsense story and its sequels—MARY POPPINS COMES BACK, MARY POPPINS OPENS THE DOOR, and MARY POPPINS IN THE PARK—are favorite reading-aloud books equally enjoyed by girls and boys.

129. CHARLOTTE'S WEB   Harper & Row
     E. B. White
     Illustrated by Garth Williams

Here is that rare book, enthusiastically received and reviewed by both children and adults. The secret lies in the lucid style of that master stylist, E. B. White, and the unique story he tells of Wilbur the silly pig and Charlotte the spider, his faithful friend. When Wilbur hears about the fall butchering he has a pig-brand of hysterics until Charlotte promises to save him. Her methods bring utter confusion to the farm families responsible for Wilbur and intense satisfaction to the smug pig. Wilbur is saved, but Charlotte's death, if biologically sound, is indubitably sad. This combination of hilarity and compassion is good therapy and superb storytelling.

130. LITTLE HOUSE IN THE BIG WOODS   Harper & Row
     Laura Ingalls Wilder
     Illustrated by Garth Williams

An authentic story of a pioneer childhood in the Wisconsin woods and first of a series based upon memories of the author's own experiences. Together, these stories of Laura Ingalls, her family, and friends form a vivid chronicle of life in the early days of the Middle West. The series includes FARMER BOY, LITTLE HOUSE ON THE PRAIRIE, ON THE BANKS OF PLUM CREEK, BY THE SHORES OF SILVER LAKE, LONG WINTER, LITTLE TOWN ON THE PRAIRIE, THESE HAPPY GOLDEN YEARS.

MYTHOLOGY, FOLKLORE, AND FAIRY TALES

131. ANDERSEN'S FAIRY TALES   Grosset & Dunlap
    Hans Christian Andersen
    Illustrated by Arthur Szyk
Andersen was the most famous creator of fairy tales. He could discover a story in such inanimate objects as a tin soldier, a darning needle, or a broom; he could also write of such uncommon things as snow queens, mermaids, ice maidens, an ugly duckling, and a princess who could feel a pea through twenty mattresses and twenty feather beds. Another good edition is: IT'S PERFECTLY TRUE, illustrated by Richard Bennett, translated by Paul Leyssac (Harcourt Brace Jovanovich).

132. STORIES OF THE GODS AND HEROES   Dial
    Sally Benson
    Illustrated by Steele Savage
Primitive man with childlike simplicity personified the mighty forces of nature and created stories about Apollo, the sun god, Athene, the goddess of wisdom, and Persephone, who was taken to Hades' realm. To the child, such myths are almost as entrancing as fairy tales, and the gods and goddesses become acquaintances to greet with pleasure when they appear in later reading. This edition is based on Thomas Bulfinch's AGE OF FABLE. Handsome, full-page colored lithographs are noteworthy in Ingri and Edgar Parin d'Aulaire's BOOK OF GREEK MYTHS (Doubleday).

133. PECOS BILL   Whitman
    James Cloyd Bowman
    Illustrated by Laura Bannon
Cleverest and mightiest of all cowboys, Pecos Bill is the mythical hero of tales of achievement, related with sturdy humor around prairie camp fires in frontier days. Accepted as American folklore, this collection of tall tales has been appropriately illustrated in color and black and white.

134. THE KING'S DRUM AND OTHER AFRICAN STORIES
                                           Harcourt Brace Jovanovich

Harold Courlander
Illustrated by Enrico Arno

A collection of African folk tales from the vast region south of the Sahara. Although animals are the primary characters, their antics invariably relate to some human condition of tribal society. The stories are marked by subtle humor, pathos, sly trickery, cruelty, honor, justice, and courage.

135. TALES FROM THE ARABIAN NIGHTS   Doubleday
    Retold from the original Arabic by H. J. Dawood
    Illustrated by Ed Young

Among the tales in this fresh, new translation are the ever-popular "Aladdin," "Ali Baba and the Forty Thieves," and "Sinbad the Sailor." Attractive full color illustrations. Another edition is ARABIAN NIGHTS, illustrated by Earle Goodenow (Grosset & Dunlap).

136. THUNDER OF THE GODS   Holt, Rinehart and Winston
    Dorothy Hosford
    Illustrated by C. and G. Louden

Boys and girls respond to the rugged quality of the Norse myths, tales of Odin, Baldur, Thor, and Loki. In this edition Dorothy Hosford retells them with strength and clarity, retaining their dramatic nature and infusing them with a rare understanding of the early civilization which first created them.

137. SOME MERRY ADVENTURES OF ROBIN HOOD   Scribner's
    Howard Pyle
    Illustrated by the author

Adapted from the old ballads, Robin Hood remains the children's favorite hero tale. Wrongfully deprived of his lands and title, Robin Hood, the Earl of Huntington, gathers about him a band of followers as stalwart as himself. In Sherwood Forest they wage war upon the cruel and greedy, right the wrongs of the poor, settle old scores in dashing style, and are eventually pardoned by the king. Their adventures, daring, humorous, and sometimes romantic, are very popular with children. This edition is a shorter version of Pyle's classic, THE ADVENTURES OF ROBIN HOOD, published in 1883. A distinguished edition using the original ballad form, SONG OF ROBIN HOOD (Houghton Mifflin), by Anne Malcolmson, has black-and-white illustrations, beautiful in design, by Virginia Lee Burton.

138. WHEN SHLEMIEL WENT TO WARSAW AND
   OTHER STORIES   Farrar, Straus & Giroux
   Isaac Bashevis Singer
   Translated by the author and Elizabeth Shub
   Illustrated by Margot Zemach
Eight tales, inspired by traditional Jewish folklore, offer fine entertainment for the whole family. Witty sketches.

POETRY

139. BOOK OF AMERICANS   Holt, Rinehart and Winston
   Rosemary Carr Benét and Stephen Vincent Benét
   Illustrated by Charles Child
From Christopher Columbus, the Pilgrims, and Miles Standish to the Wright brothers, Teddy Roosevelt, and Woodrow Wilson, these humorous poems highlight American history with uncanny skill. Some of the sketches are exceedingly funny, a few of them are serious and moving, and every one of them reveals the man with remarkable insight and completeness. This is a lively commentary on American history.

140. PEACOCK PIE   Knopf
   Walter De La Mare
   Illustrated by Barbara Cooney
Not since William Blake has anyone given us poetry for children of the quality of Walter De La Mare's. Admitting that even in his books for children there is much that is too enigmatic for them to understand, there still remains a rich residue of poetry they thoroughly enjoy. Full of fairy lore, a curious blend of reality and fantasy, ending often with a question unanswered or a mystery unsolved, these poems tease the imagination even while their melodies sing in the memory. Here is poetry that should be read aloud, heard and heard again, before it is fully savored. It is poetry to grow on.

141. FAVORITE POEMS OLD AND NEW   Doubleday
     Helen Ferris, compiler
     Illustrated by Leonard Weisgard
A rich and substantial anthology which captures varied moods and
themes and includes many old favorites as well as recent poets.
Illustrated with black-and-white stylized drawings.

142. PIPING DOWN THE VALLEYS WILD   Delacorte
     Nancy Larrick, editor
     Illustrated by Ellen Raskin
"From their earliest years children respond to poetry. The youngster
who continues to hear poetry as he grows up is fortunate, indeed.
When he listens to musical language and is stirred by word pictures,
he learns to observe his own world more clearly because he has fresh
glimpses through the eyes of a poet." In this spirit Nancy Larrick
introduces her distinguished anthology.

143. ONE AT A TIME   Little, Brown
     David McCord
     Illustrated by Henry B. Kane
David McCord is an experienced writer of verse for adults, and this
book of his collected poems for the young is a very choice addition to
the children's poetry shelf. The moods range from pure nonsense to
quiet reflection. The lilt of the verses is varied and musical.

144. WHERE THE SIDEWALK ENDS   Harper & Row
     Shel Silverstein
     Illustrated by the author
Funny, nonsensical, at times irreverent, sometimes almost profound
—here are poems about a Hug O' War instead of tug o' war, about a
boy who turns into a TV set, about Sarah Cynthia Sylvia Stout who
will not take the garbage out. Pen and ink sketches perfectly match the
spirit of the verses. All ages.

145. SMALL POEMS   Farrar, Straus & Giroux
     Valerie Worth
     Illustrated by Natalie Babbitt
Porches, sun, jewels, raw carrots, a frog, crickets—these are a few of
the subjects poetically considered in this lovely collection of simple
but vivid poems. Further fresh observations of everyday objects can

be found also in MORE SMALL POEMS and STILL MORE SMALL POEMS. In each volume Natalie Babbitt's small sketches are the just-right accompaniments.

BIOGRAPHY

146. BENJAMIN WEST AND HIS CAT GRIMALKIN

Bobbs-Merrill

Marguerite Henry
Illustrated by Wesley Dennis

A boy who found his colors in the earth, who made his brushes from his cat's tail, and who used poplar board for paper, grew up to be called the "Father of American Painting." However, it took a meeting of the entire Quaker community to decide whether the young lad should be permitted to pursue the doubtful art of picture-making. This story of the boyhood of Benjamin West is written with an appreciation of the life, the customs, and the simple pleasures of the early Pennsylvania Quakers.

147. AMERICA'S ETHAN ALLEN

Houghton Mifflin

Stewart Holbrook
Illustrated by Lynd Ward

A backwoods boy in a rough and tough region, during a rough and tough period, Ethan Allen proved his courage and the staunchness of his spirit. His was the driving force in founding the independent republic of Vermont, and, as leader of the Green Mountain Boys, it was he who planned the capture of Fort Ticonderoga. This is an exciting historical biography. The handsome pictures of Lynd Ward reflect the robust spirit of the period and illustrate the text with artistic power and deep feeling.

148. A PRAIRIE BOY'S SUMMER

Houghton Mifflin

William Kurelek
Illustrated by the author

This is the handsome companion to the author-illustrator's A PRAIRIE BOY'S WINTER. Together they present a nostalgic look at life in the thirties on a farm in Canada. Summer for William and his brother and sisters started with the end of school. There were numerous chores to be done but there were pleasures, too. Affectionate and compelling paintings by a distinguished Canadian primitive artist. All ages.

149. ME AND WILLIE AND PA   Simon & Schuster
    F. N. Monjo
    Illustrated by Douglas Gorsline
The personal side of Abraham Lincoln's years as President is narrated as his son, Tad, might have observed it. Great events in our country from 1861–65 should be easy for children to remember when presented in this pleasant manner. The author truly gives life to the Lincoln family. The illustrations resemble steel engravings of the period.

150. RASCAL   Dutton
    Sterling North
    Illustrated by John Schoenherr
The author tells his own story of one unforgettable childhood year when he found a tiny raccoon in the woods and brought it home to become his inseparable companion. This distinctive autobiography offers delightful humor, a rare feeling for wildlife and the outdoors, and wonderfully warm characterizations of the motherless Sterling and his intellectual and preoccupied father. Its greatest appeal is for eleven-year-olds and through the early teens.

For Children 12, 13, and 14

FICTION

151. LITTLE WOMEN   Collins
     Louisa M. Alcott
     IIlustrated by Tasha Tudor

Good stories of family life are always popular, but none has ever been more universally beloved than this classic written over a century ago. The four March girls and their mother are genuine people, delightfully individual. Children follow their struggles, fun, tragedy. amd romance with as much interest today as they ever did. Jo is not only a favorite character but stands for the self-reliant, impulsive, enterprising young woman the modern girl admires. Preadolescents also are attracted to this story. Another recommended edition is: LITTLE WOMEN, illustrated by Jessie Willcox Smith (Little, Brown).

152. THE BOOK OF THREE   Holt, Rinehart and Winston
     Lloyd Alexander

"There are time when the seeking counts more than the finding." This philosophy of the author pervades this tale of Taran, Assistant Pig-Keeper in the mythical kingdom of Prydain, who, in his search for the oracular pig Hen Wen, becomes involved in a hazardous mission to save his country from the forces of evil. Inspired by Welsh legend and mythology, this well-written fantasy is the first title in the chronicle of Prydain. It is followed by THE BLACK CAULDRON, THE CASTLE OF LLYR, TARAN WANDERER, and THE HIGH KING (*Newbery Medal*, 1969).

153. TUCK EVERLASTING   Farrar, Straus & Giroux
     Natalie Babbitt

During a few hot August days strange, frightening and wonderful things happen in and near the village of Treegap. Winnie Foster, longing for an exciting interlude in her prim, ordered life, ventures into the woods and meets the Tucks, an unusual family who have received everlasting life after drinking from a spring deep in the forest. Trying to protect their dangerous secret, the Tucks take Winnie to their home. At first the girl wants to escape but soon she becomes closely attached to the family; however, tragedy hits when an unscrupulous stranger arrives. Eventually there is a great lesson in trust and love. Beautifully written, this story invites rereading and discussion. It can be enjoyed by ten- and eleven-year-olds as well. This talented author has written a number of other stories with ingenious plots, pleasing fluent language, and moving images.

154. THE INCREDIBLE JOURNEY   Atlantic-Little, Brown
     Sheila Burnford
     Illustrated by Carl Burger

The loyalty of animals to home and master is a familiar theme. But for sheer inventiveness, this story of a young Labrador retriever, an old bullterrier, and a Siamese cat on a 250-mile trek through the Canadian wilderness is exceptional. These pampered house pets, each in his own way, share the hazards of the journey. Even the aloof and independent cat brings her kill to the old bullterrier after he is injured in a battle with a bear, and each resists the human beings who try to detain them from reaching their former home. The author's intimate knowledge of the ways of these animals gives credibility to a tale of intense drama and suspense, while the disciplined style makes it a perfect read-aloud book.

155. THE WHITE MOUNTAINS   Macmillan
     John Christopher

This science fantasy is set a hundred years in the future. It is a powerfully told story of three boys who flee across Europe to the White Mountains, a natural barrier against the Tripods, merciless creatures who seek to control men's minds and make them docile slaves. This is the first book in an adventure-filled trilogy which tells of human efforts to discover the vulnerability of their strange enemies and to defeat them. The other titles are THE CITY OF GOLD AND LEAD and POOL OF FIRE.

156. THE WONDERFUL WINTER   Dutton
    Marchette Chute
    Illustrated by Grace Golden

Young Sir Robin Wakefield had a hard enough time with his three severe aunts; but when an unpleasant tutor was added to his trials, the boy and his dog set off for London. Half-starved, he finally blundered into Mr. Shakespeare's own theatre, where he was discovered by the poet, gently cared for, and taken into the home of actor John Heminges. Mrs. Heminges, the children, and even the boy apprentice all took kindly to Robin. He in turn blossomed in the warm, affectionate, and lively household. Eventually Robin was pressed into bit parts in the theatre, to his great delight, for he loved both Shakespeare and the plays. But by the end of his wonderful winter, Robin knew he must return to home and responsibilities. There is a triumphant homecoming and promise of a bright future for this winning young hero. A delightful picture of many aspects of Elizabethan London and the theatre of Will Shakespeare.

157. WHERE THE LILIES BLOOM   Lippincott
    Vera and Bill Cleaver

Set in the Great Smokies, this is the taut, realistic story of fourteen-year-old Mary Call Luther's proud and independent efforts to keep her orphaned brother and sisters together without help from the outside. In a sequel, TRIAL VALLEY, Mary Call, now sixteen, finds her personal values and her future deeply affected by an abandoned child and by the romantic attentions of two very different young men.

158. ADVENTURES OF TOM SAWYER   Harper & Row
    Samuel L. Clemens (pseud. Mark Twain)
    Illustrated by Worth Brehm

In TOM SAWYER juvenile realism crossed the tracks for the first time to give children a casual glimpse of the seamy side of life. Tom's adventures involve Aunt Polly and her church-going friends on the one hand, Huck and his disreputable father on the other, and a hair-raising tragedy in the cave. Besides the absurd and hilarious episodes in this story, the mystery in which the boys become involved keeps this book a favorite with each succeeding generation. First published in 1876. Another attractive edition is: ADVENTURES OF TOM SAWYER, illustrated by Donald McKay (Grosset & Dunlap).

159. CHRISTMAS CAROL Lippincott
Charles Dickens
Illustrated by Arthur Rackham
Ebenezer Scrooge, Tiny Tim, Bob Cratchit, and all the other characters of this well-known tale are as beloved today as they were over a century ago when this story first appeared.

160. THE TWENTY-ONE BALLOONS Viking
William Pène DuBois
Illustrated by the author
Weary of teaching mathematics to the young, Professor Sherman equips a balloon and flies off in search of adventure. His journey ends suddenly when a hungry gull punctures the balloon and forces him down on the volcanic island of Krakatoa, rich in diamonds, unusual inhabitants, and explosive potentialities. A rare and imaginative pseudo-scientific tale told with great good humor and profusely illustrated by the author-artist. *Newbery Medal*, 1948.

161. JOHNNY TREMAIN Houghton Mifflin
Esther Forbes
Illustrated by Lynd Ward
Revolutionary days in Boston found Johnny, a boy of thirteen, apprenticed to a silversmith. Accidentally maimed for life and unable to follow his trade, Johnny was caught up in the struggle for liberty. The author has a remarkable talent for transporting the reader to the scene; the wharves and streets of Boston, the Tea Party and what led up to it, and the fighting at Lexington and Concord are before the eyes as though the intervening years had been rolled aside. *Newbery Medal*, 1944.

162. MY SIDE OF THE MOUNTAIN Dutton
Jean George
Illustrated by the author
An incredible story of a modern boy's life alone in the Catskill Mountains for one year. Making his home in the hollowed trunk of a hemlock tree, Sam Gribley learns to build a fire without matches, make a deerskin suit, and cook everything from frog soup to venison steak. This competent young "Thoreau's" descriptions of unforgettable experiences in the heart of nature make the book a delightful flight from civilization.

163. JULIE OF THE WOLVES
Harper & Row

Jean C. George

This is the moving account of a thirteen-year-old Eskimo girl who faces some difficult decisions in her changing world when she is lost on the Tundra with only a wolf pack for company. There is little dialogue in the story but it is by no means slow moving. The traditional way of life of the Eskimo and the problems encountered with "civilization" are illuminated. The feel for animal life is superb. *Newbery Medal,* 1973.

164. M. C. HIGGINS, THE GREAT
Macmillan

Virginia Hamilton

Sitting atop his 40-foot pole, M. C. Higgins dreams of escape for his family from the creeping ruin of strip-mining which threatens his Ohio hill country home. Two strangers—a recorder of folk songs and a restless seventeen-year-old girl—help M. C. find the answer to this problem and deepen his awareness of himself and his racial heritage. *Newbery Medal,* 1975. Intense and involved storytelling also marks the author's ARILLA SUN DOWN (Greenwillow) which describes the struggle of a young girl, part Black, part American Indian, as she searches for self identity.

165. THE LITTLE FISHES
Houghton Mifflin

Erik Christian Haugaard
Illustrated by Milton Johnson

Homeless Guido tells his own story of his efforts to lead two younger orphans from war-torn Naples to hoped-for safety farther north. Throughout the long journey the children encounter many people, both kind and cruel. This moving narrative of World War II is unforgettable for its depiction of a large cast of characters memorably described, and Guido, who is only twelve, stands out as a child of wartime whose many hardships develop in him a deep sense of compassion for others.

166. ACROSS FIVE APRILS
Follett

Irene Hunt

Jethro Creighton is helping his mother plant potatoes on their southern Illinois farm when news comes that Fort Sumter has been fired upon. The Civil War stretches across five Aprils, from the year Jethro is nine until he is fourteen. He sees three brothers leave, one, after much soul-searching, to fight on the Confederate side. After his father's heart attack, all the farm work rests on Jethro's slender shoulders, but at the war's end, with the help of the local schoolmaster, he pursues the education he so ardently longs for. The warm family life and the characterization of each member give distinction to this book. Having heard stories of the war from her grandfather and having access to family letters and records, the author imparts an unusual sense of reality to the struggle of the Creightons during the long conflict.

167. A STRANGER CAME ASHORE   Harper & Row
Mollie Hunter

Robbie, with the help of his teacher, part wizard, foils the evil intentions of the stranger, Finn Learson, toward his bonny sister, Elspeth. A gripping tale based on the Great Selkie legends of the Shetland Islands. In a number of her stories Mollie Hunter does a masterful job of mingling legends of long ago with present-day mystery. The author has also written powerful historical fiction.

168. SMOKY, THE COWHORSE   Scribner's
Will James
Illustrated by the author

Because Will James was a cowboy and knew a horse as only a cowboy could, this is one of the great stories of its kind, as well as a true picture of ranch life in the West. *Newbery Medal, 1927.*

169. RIFLES FOR WATIE   Crowell
Harold Keith

To sixteen-year-old Jeff Bussey the Civil War promised to be a grand soldierly adventure. But the grueling years of small hardships and grave dangers, together with a strange set of circumstances which had Jeff serving in the Southern as well as the Northern armies, give the boy a new sympathy with all victims of war. A stirring and enlightening historical tale which does full justice to the Northern and Southern points of view. *Newbery Medal, 1958.*

170. BIG RED   Holiday
Jim Kjelgaard
Illustrated by Bob Kuhn

Between Danny and his father there was the warmth of sympathetic understanding, but between Danny and the Irish setter which was given him for training there was devotion that needed no words for expression. This is an exceptional story of the simultaneous development of a champion and a skilled trainer of champions and of the way they met Big Majesty, the bear which had long reigned supreme in the Wintapi wilderness.

171. ... AND NOW MIGUEL   Crowell
   Joseph Krumgold
   Illustrated by Jean Charlot
A regional story of deeply-rooted family life in New Mexico, where everyone from grandfather to uncles is a sheepraiser on land owned for generations by this family of Spanish descent. But this is also Miguel's story. For at twelve a boy is thinking of being a man, and to Miguel this would happen when he went with the men who take the sheep to the Sangre de Cristo Mountains for summer pasture. In telling how Miguel got his wish, the author shows a penetrating and perceptive understanding of a twelve-year-old boy. *Newbery Medal,* 1954.

172. MEET THE AUSTINS   Vanguard
   Madeleine L'Engle
Modern family life in a lively and sometimes turbulent household of four children from five to fifteen, as seen by Vicky, age twelve. There is laughter, tragedy, and adjustment to living with a spoiled, suddenly orphaned girl of ten, who is befriended by the Austins. Told with zest and understanding not only of growing children but of what makes a warm and loving family. A WIND IN THE DOOR (Farrar, Straus & Giroux) is a sequel.

173. A WRINKLE IN TIME   Farrar, Straus & Giroux
   Madeleine L'Engle
The discerning reader who likes to be transported from the world of reality to the strange and mysterious will find this fantasy of space and time both original and fascinating. A brother and sister, together with a friend, go in search of their scientist father who was lost while engaged in secret work for the government on the tesseract program. A tesseract is a wrinkle in time. The father is a prisoner on a forbidding planet, and after awesome and terrifying experiences, he is rescued,

and the little group returns safely to Earth and home. *Newbery Medal*, 1963. Followed by A SWIFTLY TILTING PLANET.

174. ISLAND OF THE BLUE DOLPHINS　　　　Houghton Mifflin
　　　Scott O'Dell
Because her brother had missed the ship that was taking their tribe to the mainland, Karana, a young Indian girl, remains with him. After her brother's death she lives alone for eighteen years on this wildly beautiful, treeless island off the coast of California. The struggle for survival is told in grim, realistic detail, alleviated by Karana's ability to find some comfort, beauty, and a measure of happiness in her solitary life. Based on the few facts known about an actual experience, the story is told with stark simplicity beautifully fitted to such a deeply moving experience. *Newbery Medal*, 1961. Further compelling reading can be found in the sequel, ZIA, illustrated by Ted Lewin.

175. THE MASTER PUPPETEER　　　　　　　　　Crowell
　　　Katherine Paterson
　　　Illustrated by Haru Wells
Jiro, runaway son of a puppet-maker, and Kinski, son of the most feared and renowned of all puppeteers of ancient Osaka, Japan, learn to master the art of the puppet theater amid mystery and intrigue. A National Book Award winning story.

176. THE YEARLING　　　　　　　　　　　　Scribner's
　　　Marjorie Kinnan Rawlings
　　　Illustrated by N. C. Wyeth
This sensitive story of a lonely little boy, Jody, in the poverty-stricken wastelands of Florida, is enlivened by an epic bear hunt, the boy's delight in his pet fawn, and his pride in the triumphs of his pint-sized father over their brawny neighbors. The final tragedy turns upon Jody's inability to face the cruel reality that his deer is destroying the family's scanty food supply and must be killed. The father's understanding and love make this story of growing up a little masterpiece.

177. THE WITCH OF BLACKBIRD POND　　　Houghton Mifflin
　　　Elizabeth Speare
Headstrong and undisciplined, Barbados-bred Kit Tyler is an embarrassment to her Puritan relatives, and her sincere attempts to aid a reputed witch soon bring her to trial as a suspect. This distinguished

story with its seventeenth-century background offers an absorbing historical romance of the tragic witch-hunting days in early Connecticut. *Newbery Medal,* 1959.

178. TREASURE ISLAND   Macmillan
    Robert Louis Stevenson
    Illustrated by John Falter
A dying pirate in a lonely inn starts young Jim Hawkins on a remarkable quest for buried treasure. This classic tale of the sea and hidden gold has no equal in adventure stories for young people. Originally published in 1882.

179. DAWN WIND   Walck
    Rosemary Sutcliff
    Illustrated by Charles Keeping
Turbulent England during the invasion of the barbaric Saxon hordes is recreated with superb historical imagination. After the last savage battle, a fourteen-year-old boy becomes a thrall with a slave collar about his neck. Given his freedom after twelve years of serfdom, he goes in search of the half-starved waif of a girl he had earlier befriended. But most important of all, he feels the first breath of the dawn wind which promises the end of strife and a peaceful Christian homeland once again. The narrative is handled with unusual skill by an English author who has won the Carnegie Medal, which is similar to our Newbery Medal.

180. ROLL OF THUNDER, HEAR MY CRY   Dial
    Mildred D. Taylor
Strengthened by black pride, love of land, and deep family loyalty, the Logans, a black family living in Mississippi at the height of the Depression are able to face prejudice and discrimination. This tense and absorbing story concentrates primarily on the children and young people. *Newbery Medal,* 1977.

181. THE HOBBIT   Houghton Mifflin
    J. R. R. Tolkien
    Illustrated by the author
It was some years before the children of the United States took to THE HOBBIT. Now they are devotees like their older brothers and sisters. In this book, as well as in the trilogy of THE RING, the fairy tale turns into an allegory of Good and Evil, but this disturbs neither

the reader nor the hilarious action of the tale. The first chapter is a masterpiece of confusion. The wizard Gandalf and innumerable dwarfs, descending upon respectable well-to-do Bilbo Baggins, demand food, drink and his aid on a perilous adventure. Bilbo has no intention of going, but he does and becomes a hero in spite of himself. Humor, action, unique characters, and compelling style make THE HOBBIT a must for good readers—children and adults.

182. BANNER IN THE SKY   Lippincott
      James Ramsey Ullman

Not only does this story provide young readers with thrilling action, but it gives them a memorable picture of the stern discipline, physical and moral, that goes into the making of a Swiss mountain guide. Young Rudi, though forced to work in a hotel kitchen, is determined to become a famous guide like his father. Secretly he cherishes the ambition to scale the Citadel, where his father lost his life, and to plant his father's red shirt on the pinnacle. Rudi's ups and downs are chiefly downs until he submits to rigorous training.

183. THE LONER   McKay
      Ester Wier
      Illustrated by Christine Price

A young migratory worker, without home or identity, is taken in by a lonely old woman, the "boss" of a Montana sheep ranch. He earns his name, David, after killing a grizzly bear, his Goliath, and after some time he becomes convinced that the ranch is his home. One dramatic episode, the death of a girl caught in a farm machine, is not glossed over, but neither is it morbidly emphasized. This is a fine, realistic story, sensitively told, and one in which both people and animals are strongly portrayed. For any adolescent who feels he is a "loner" this story will have special significance.

184. THESE HAPPY GOLDEN YEARS   Harper & Row
      Laura Ingalls Wilder
      Illustrated by Garth Williams

The author has written many of the experiences of her own childhood in this outstanding pioneer series, which begins with LITTLE HOUSE IN THE BIG WOODS for youngest readers and concludes with this story of the heroine's marriage after a year of teaching. These books are a valuable contribution to the historical fiction of America's growth. Titles for the complete series are given in 130.

MYTHS AND LEGENDARY HERO TALES

185. CHILDREN OF ODIN
Macmillan

Padraic Colum

Illustrated by Willy Pogany

The Norse myths of Thor and Odin, of Loki the mischievous one, and of Iduna and her golden apples are retold in simple, rhythmic prose. Boys and girls like the strength and vigor of these old tales, and, because Padraic Colum has done his work directly from the Eddas, he has retained these qualities.

186. MYTHOLOGY
Little, Brown

Edith Hamilton

Illustrated by Steele Savage

A distinguished classical scholar presents a lucid, readable introduction to the theogony, myths, and epic tales of ancient Greece and Rome, including also a brief section on Norse mythology.

187. THE ILIAD OF HOMER
Walck

Homer

Retold by Barbara Leonie Picard

Illustrated by Joan Kiddell-Monroe

Here is an exceptionally well done retelling of Homer's epic poem, including a prologue, epilog, and a glossary of names.

188. KING ARTHUR AND HIS KNIGHTS OF THE ROUND TABLE
Grosset & Dunlap

Sir Thomas Malory

Edited by Sidney Lanier

Illustrated by Florian

The fine ideals of chivalry and of disinterested service to a great cause are represented by the Knights of the Round Table. While their adventurous exploits provide the thrill of difficulties overcome and battles won, youth finds inspiration to be courageous, loyal, and faithful to a trust. This edition follows Malory's MORTE D'ARTHUR closely.

189. PAUL BUNYAN Harcourt Brace Jovanovich
     Esther Shephard
     Illustrated by Rockwell Kent
Tall tales of the mighty exploits of the legendary hero of American lumberjacks; of Teeny, his daughter; Babe, his great blue ox; and other woodsmen who range the forests from Maine to the Northwest. The robust vigor of the tales is graphically reproduced in the illustrations by Rockwell Kent. Another edition for the younger reader is OL' PAUL: THE MIGHTY LOGGER (Holiday) by Glen Rounds.

190. LAND OF HEROES: A RETELLING OF THE
     KALEVALA Atheneum
     Ursula Synge
The Kalevala—Land of Heroes—Finland's national epic first appeared as song cycles about Vainamoinen the Wise Singer, Ilmarinen the Smith, and Lemminkainer the Scapegrace, and their feud with Mistress Louhi, sorcere_s of the cold, cold North. This lyrical prose retelling of the song cycles retains the vitality and magic of the originals.

POETRY

191. AN INHERITANCE OF POETRY Houghton Mifflin
     Gladys Adshead and Annis Duff, compilers
     Illustrated by Nora S. Unwin
This choice collection of poems is designed for family use, which explains why many of the poems have appeal for adolescents and adults. There are, nevertheless, exquisite selections for children, and the book makes a delightful addition to family reading.

192. POEMS OF EMILY DICKINSON Crowell
     Emily Dickinson

Selected by Helen Plotz
Drawings by Robert Kipniss

Prefaced by a perceptive introduction to the life of Emily Dickinson, here is a generous sampling of the nineeenth-century American poetess's sensitive expression of nature, love, the inner life, immortality, and the world around her.

193. REFLECTIONS ON A GIFT OF WATERMELON
     PICKLE ... AND OTHER MODERN VERSE

Lothrop, Lee & Shepard

Stephen Dunning, Edward Lueders, High Smith, compilers
Illustrated with photographs

Stimulating modern verse on an immense variety of subjects ranging from nature to moods and to reflections and observations of the world we live in. There is a brief provocative introduction on the reading of poetry for enjoyment, followed by over a hundred poems of delightful diversity and distinctive quality.

194. YOU COME TOO   Holt, Rinehart & Winston

Robert Frost
Illustrated by Thomas Nason

More than any other poet, Robert Frost speaks for America with the voice and cadence of Americans. This is one reason why children should encounter his poetry early. The poet has made this a grateful task by choosing from his vast store this special selection of poems for children and youth. They may begin these poems at five, and they will still cherish them at eighty-five. For in spite of their seeming simplicity, they are rich in secondary meanings that do not occur to the reader at first. Meanwhile, this selection of Robert Frost's poems will give young readers a rare encounter with authentic poetry of high order.

195. DON'T YOU TURN BACK   Knopf

Langston Hughes
Lee Bennett Hopkins, editor
Illustrated by Ann Grifalconi

Bold, spare woodcuts perfectly balance the strength and simplicity of these short selections taken from the work of a distinguished black poet. This can be shared with younger children.

196. ZERO MAKES ME HUNGRY   Lothrop, Lee & Shepard
Edward Lueders and Primus St. John, editors
Illustrated by John Reuter-Pacyna
Twentieth-century poetry makes an eloquent statement in this superb collection of poems with contemporary impact and sharp insights. Rainbow-colored free form accents and use of color in print add to the attractiveness of this volume.

197. IMAGINATION'S OTHER PLACE   Crowell
Helen Plotz, compiler
Illustrated by Clare Leighton
This unique anthology for older children, youth, and adults is devoted to the poetry of science and mathematics, and all the sciences from astronomy to surgery are here. Each group opens with a relevant selection from the Bible. But this is not a solemn book. There are occasional limericks or nonsense verses, dramatic poems, and pure lyrics; and every poem has been chosen with a discriminating eye and ear for authentic poetry. Clare Leighton's illustrations and the beautiful format of the book add to the delight of the reader in exploring this treasure.

198. THIS WAY, DELIGHT   Pantheon
Sir Herbert Read, compiler
Illustrated by Juliet Kepes
"Poetry should be a deep delight,' says Sir Herbert Read in a brief essay at the end of this distinguished anthology. Although poems written primarily for children are not found in these one hundred poems, which range from Shakespeare to Dylan Thomas, all the poems are within the young person's ability to understand and enjoy. The design, illustration, and format set a high standard of excellence in keeping with the content.

199. STARS TO-NIGHT   Macmillan
Sara Teasdale
Illustrated by Dorothy Lathrop
Lyric poetry about stars and night, coupled with Dorothy Lathrop's equally imaginative drawings, make this a choice book to read and to look at. Special favorites with children are: "Stars," "Night," "February Twilight," "Falling Star," "Winter Moon," "The Coin," and "Redbirds."

BIOGRAPHY AND TRAVEL

200. PATRICK HENRY: FIREBRAND OF
THE REVOLUTION
Little, Brown
Nardi Reeder Campion
Illustrated by Victor Mays

A lackadaisical youngster and an indifferent student, Patrick Henry, was spurred to heights of patriotism and achievement during the American Revolution by his domestic responsibility and growing concern for his country. Well documented and written with disarming simplicity, as well as distinction, this book creates a stirring picture of an emerging nation and its leaders.

201. ANDREW JACKSON
Houghton Mifflin
Margaret Coit
Illustrated by Milton Johnson

The tough, peppery frontiersman who became seventh president of the United States of America comes alive in this vivid and enlightening biography, which shows why "Jacksonian Democracy" became a part of our heritage.

202. TOM PAINE, REVOLUTIONARY
Scribner's
Olivia E. Coolidge

A carefully researched, perceptive biography of a controversial man who devoted himself to the American Revolution, the rights of man, and the reformation of religion. Another moving biography is the author's GANDHI (Houghton Mifflin).

203. DANIEL BOONE
Viking
James Daugherty
Illustrated by the author

Upon the author's return from a trip through the Cumberlands, the Smokies, and Boonesborough, he was inspired to tell Boone's story again because he believes that Boone and "his tough true breed are calling cross a hundred years to young America." The spirit of the lusty, vigorous new country is in the rhythmic prose as well as in the illustrations. *Newbery Medal*, 1940.

204. LEADER BY DESTINY
Harcourt Brace Jovanovich
Jeanette Eaton

Illustrated by Jack Manley Rose

This definitive biography of Washington for young people makes use of recent research findings to create a vivid picture of a remarkable man. Revealing episodes in his early career show him sometimes humiliated and close to disgrace but struggling on to become a disciplined leader of men. The title of the book is also its theme— Washington called by destiny to play a role for which he had little taste. He forced himself into the leader he was called upon to be.

205. W. E. B. DU BOIS   Crowell
Virginia Hamilton
Illustrated with photographs
Virginia Hamilton grew up in a household where her father would never allow a word to be spoken against the marvelous Dr. Du Bois and his "Crises" magazine. The author says, "He was a black man and he was a great man who belonged to me and all those like me. No wonder, then, that the writing of this biography seemed so natural, like the completion of a familiar idea." The author's notes, the extensive bibliography, and the careful index indicate the research she put into this dignified and balanced life story.

206. THE ENDLESS STEPPE: GROWING UP IN RUSSIA   Crowell
Esther Hautzig
In June, 1941 ten-year-old Esther Rudomin's life amid a busy, loving, well-ordered Polish–Jewish household was drastically changed when the family, termed "capitalists and therefore enemies of the people," was herded into cattle cars and taken on a long, hard journey to Rubtsovsk, Siberia, where they became slave laborers for five years. This autobiographical account reveals the magnificent spirit that triumphed over the privations and degradations suffered. An outstanding story which has a great message for the heart and the mind.

207. KON-TIKI   Rand McNally
Thor Heyerdahl
Translated by F. H. Lyon
A spell-binding chronicle of the voyage from Peru to the Polynesian Islands taken by the author and five companions on a balsa-wood raft. The grandeur and beauty of the ever-changing sea and sky as well as the countless dangers which were their daily fare are recounted with

seldom-matched skill. This memorable book, translated from the Norwegian, has many of the qualities of a classic.

208. CARRY ON, MR. BOWDITCH   Houghton Mifflin
   Jean Lee Latham
   Illustrated by John O'Hara Cosgrove II
A lively biography of a mathematician and astronomer who, before he was thirty, wrote "The American Practical Navigator," still a standard text in the U.S. Naval Academy. An undersized and undernourished boy in a poverty-stricken home, Nathaniel Bowditch had to leave school when he was ten. Apprenticed to a ship chandler in Salem, Massachusetts, during the days of the sailing ships, he spent his nights reading and studying by himself and later, when he went to sea, applied his knowledge to navigation. An inspiring and animated account of a man who with perseverance and singleness of purpose achieved success. *Newbery Medal,* 1956.

209. I, CHARLOTTE FORTEN, BLACK AND FREE   Crowell
   Polly Longsworth
Charlotte Forten, a rich, free black girl whose grandfather was James Forten, the sailmaker, attended school in New England and came in contact with men like Whittier, Phillips, Douglass and Garrison. Written in first person, this fine biography is based on Ray Allen Billington's edition of Charlotte's diary. Another interesting biography by Polly Longsworth is EMILY DICKINSON: HER LETTER TO THE WORLD.

210. ABE LINCOLN GROWS UP   Harcourt Brace Jovanovich
   Carl Sandburg
   Illustrated by James Daugherty
This biography includes the first twenty-seven chapters from the author's ABRAHAM LINCOLN, THE PRAIRIE YEARS. It covers the boyhood and youth of Lincoln, which Sandburg has recreated out of his own feeling for an understanding of the prairie background from which Lincoln came.

211. AMOS FORTUNE, FREE MAN   Dutton
   Elizabeth Yates
   Illustrated by Nora Unwin
Born a free man, the son of an African chief, Amos Fortune was sold

into slavery and brought to this country in 1725. Becoming a tanner by trade, he bought his freedom and, through hard work and sacrifice, that of others. At his death he was a respected citizen of Jaffrey, New Hampshire. This is the moving story not of a great statesman or leader but of a simple man, whose deep religious feeling and dedication to the fight for freedom make him an impressive individual. *Newbery Medal,* 1951.

The Artist and Childrens Books

Much of the poetry of childhood depends upon the great talent and artistic insight that characterize illustrations for children's stories. The following eighteen pages contain black-and-white reproductions of some of the best present-day picture material for children's books. They are included in this bibliography through the kind permission of the artists and their publishers: Blackie & Son, Ltd.; Coward-McCann-Geoghegan, Inc.; Thomas Y. Crowell Co.; Doubleday and Co., Inc.; Farrar Straus & Giroux, Inc.; Harper & Row, Publishers; Houghton-Mifflin Co.; Macmillan Publishing Co.; Charles Scribner's Sons; Vanguard Press, Inc.; The Viking Press, Inc.; and World's Work, Ltd.

MARCIA BROWN

Once a Mouse   Scribner's
Adapted by the illustrator   Illustration © 1961 by Marcia Brown

Marcia Brown is one of the most versatile of modern artists. She adapts her style to the mood and content of the story. The sturdy figure of *Dick Whittington* in earthy browns and black is precisely right for that hero. So are the flamboyant pinks for the dashing *Puss in Boots* and the delicately drawn figures in misty pastels for *The Steadfast Tin Soldier* and *Cinderella, Caldecott Medal, 1955.* But her book *Once a Mouse, Caldecott Medal, 1962*, differs from all the others. The artist has used the difficult medium of woodcuts with a posterlike effect that is boldly stylized and wonderfully interpretive of mood and action. The details in these striking pictures will reward a closer look. In rich jungle colors, the story of the rise and fall of an ungrateful mouse is as dramatically told by the pictures as by the text.

VIRGINIA LEE BURTON

Mike Mulligan and His Steam Shovel   Houghton Mifflin
By the illustrator

Virginia Lee Burton was a dancer before she was a successful author-artist. Perhaps this accounts for the swinging circular lines she uses to express action. Over and over again, the composition of her pictures follows this circular or elliptical pattern—from the forest and fights of *Robin Hood* to the evolution of a city in *The Little House*. In that book her crowding skyscrapers, elevated railroads, trolleys, and tracks do a whirling ballet in verticals and circles. Her personifications of runaway trains or plodding steam shovels follow this same pattern. And no one can personify a child's beloved machines more gaily and vividly than she.

BARBARA COONEY
Chanticleer and the Fox   Crowell
Geoffrey Chaucer, adapted by the illustrator

For *Chanticleer* Barbara Cooney has used stylized illustrations well
suited to the precise form of the fable. In strong, bold colors she has
drawn the widow and her children, their little house, farm, and all the
animals. But on Chanticleer and his smiling enemy, the fox, she has
lavished glorious colors and decorative details that highlight these
handsome, well-matched antagonists. The medieval setting of "The
Nun's Priest's Tale," from which this fable is taken, is beautifully
realized in both the pictures and text. This is a book to reread, pore
over, and cherish. *Caldecott Medal, 1959.*

JAMES DAUGHERTY
Daniel Boone   Viking
By the illustrator

James Daugherty loves the great figures and the epic sweep of American history. He writes and illustrates with a rhythmic vigor that is well suited to the lusty heroes he portrays. His pictures are crowded and sometimes confusing. Details are subordinated to a single dominant impression—stark strength or savage action or wild gaiety or surging energy. The power in James Daugherty's illustrations is compelling. They are not pretty pictures, but they are memorable. *Newbery Medal, 1940.*

WANDA GÁG

Tales from Grimm
Adapted by the illustrator

Coward-McCann-Geoghegan

Wanda Gág grew up in a family that was steeped in the folk art of the Old World. Her father painted in his spare time, and every child in the family began to draw as soon as he could hold a pencil and manage a scrap of paper. The old fairy tales she heard influenced Wanda Gág's own writing and illustrating. Both have a unique folk quality. Sturdy peasant figures appear in her pictures, and homely details of everyday living. Strong masses of blacks and whites are balanced with a rhythmic flow of lines that give to her compositions both strength and grace. Children delight in exploring her humorous details, and adults appreciate the tender beauty of her work.

THEODOR SEUSS GEISEL
The 500 Hats of Bartholomew Cubbins Vanguard
By the illustrator

Theodor Seuss Geisel, known as "Dr. Seuss," can turn humorous fantasy into beauty both in his stories and his pictures. His pop-eyed heroes, his impossible hats, fish, or birds, his stilt-loving royalty, or his wizards and nizzards have about them a beauty of line, a sudden splash of color, or a grace of movement that is utterly captivating. This is true of his landscapes as well. Seeing Theodor Geisel in his hilltop studio in California, with the city below him or the mountains, half lost in mist, above him, one finds it easy to understand how dreams might come alive for him. But nothing except his own creative genius can account of the unique quality of his nonsense, which, at its most hilarious peak, has also beauty.

NONNY HOGROGIAN
One Fine Day   Macmillan
By the illustrator

Nonny Hogrogian's illustrations are particularly notable for their
warm and witty qualities. For Sorche Nic Leodhas' Scottish folk
song, *Always Room For One More* (*Caldecott Medal, 1966*), she has
provided enchanting pen and ink drawings with chalk and color wash.
There is a sense of rhythm in the rich, sunny pictures for *Apples,* a
wordless book. The expressive crayon drawings, coupled with
delightful black and white ones, in *The Contest*, a humorous retelling
of an Armenian folktale, are another example of this gifted artist's
outstanding contributions to art for children.

EZRA JACK KEATS
The Snowy Day   Viking
By the illustrator   Illustration © 1962 by Ezra Jack Keats

Small Peter's glorious adventure playing in the winter's first deep snow is told in crisp rhythmic prose and uncluttered illustrations, which combine collage and watercolor and contrast brilliant and muted tones with rare distinction. *Caldecott Medal, 1963.*

Little Georgie lay back in the warm grass and sang his song—

New Folks co-ming, Oh my! New Folks co-ming, Oh my! New Folks co-ming, Oh my! Oh my! Oh my!

ROBERT LAWSON
Rabbit Hill   Viking
By the illustrator

Robert Lawson ranks as one of America's outstanding book illustrators for children and is an author of distinction as well. His finely detailed drawings make his every character, human or animal, a genuine personality. His humor, whether robust, as in the drawings for *Ferdinand, Ben and Me,* and *Mr. Popper's Penguins,* or delicately sensitive, as in the illustrations for *Rabbit Hill* and *They Were Strong and Good,* unfailingly interpret the spirit of the story. Mr. Lawson has illustrated some thirty books, and he is the only juvenile author-artist who has won both the *Newbery* and *Caldecott Medals.*

ROBERT McCLOSKEY
Make Way for Ducklings   Viking
By the illustrator

Lentil, the first book by the author-illustrator Robert McCloskey, was
quickly recognized as a choice bit of Ohioana. *Make Way for
Ducklings, Caldecott Medal 1941,* and the later picture stories,
Blueberries for Sal, One Morning in Maine, and *Time of Wonder,*
(*Caldecott Medal, 1958*), are similarly a part of the New England
scene. In his chronicles of Homer Price as related and pictured in
Homer Price and *Centerburg Tales,* Mr. McCloskey has created a
character as truly American as Tom Sawyer. With absolute integrity
he describes and draws what he sees and invests it with the kind of
humor and realism that children understand and persons of any age
enjoy.

MAURICE SENDAK
Little Bear   Harper & Row
By Else H. Minarik   In Great Britain: World's Work
Illustration © 1957 by Maurice Sendak

Maurice Sendak's pictures for children fall into two distinct styles.
His first illustrations for Ruth Krauss' *A Hole Is to Dig*, and for many
succeeding books, pictured the antic grace of everyday children,
cavorting like frolicsome pups. But in his own first book, *Kenny's
Window*, both story and illustrations reveal a sensitive perception of
the lonely, imaginative, inner life of children. This is evidenced again
in his beautiful, full-color pictures of moon-mad dancing children in
Janice Udry's *Moon Jumpers*. And again his illustrations for Else
Minarik's well-loved *Little Bear* books reveal the inner warmth and
love of family relations. *Nutshell Library,* with its four tiny books,
written and illustrated by Mr. Sendak, is another example of this
artist's creative gifts. Maurice Sendak well deserved his international
acclaim when he received the Hans Christian Andersen Medal in
1970, the first time an American artist was so recognized.

KATE SEREDY
The Good Master　　　　　　　　　　　　　　Viking
By the illustrator

Kate Seredy once said that as a youngster in Hungary, she was in the saddle so much of the time that she felt almost six-legged. Perhaps this helps to account for the fact that she has a special gift for depicting action both in the horses she draws with such power and the human figures. Swirling skirts, blowing draperies, the light tilt of young figures; hoofs off the ground, dust flying, or the bold stance of a spirited horse—these convey to the beholder something of the excitement of headlong action.

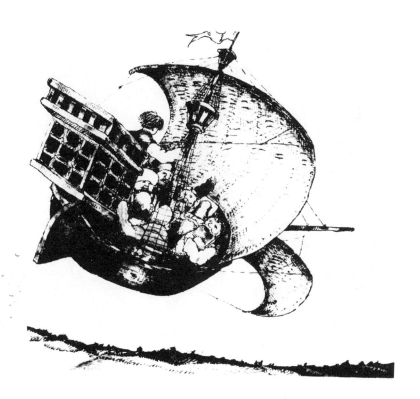

URI SHULEVITZ
The Fool of the World and the Flying Ship:
A Russian Tale   Farrar, Straus & Giroux
Arthur Ransome, reteller   Illustration © 1968 by Uri Shulevitz

Warsaw-born Uri Shulevitz has illustrated a great variety of books by
other authors as well as his own. He makes a special contribution to
the field of folklore because of his colorful, imaginative drawings often
touched with humor, as typified in this winner of the *Caldecott
Medal, 1969.*

PETER SPIER
Noah's Ark   Doubleday
By the illustrator

Amsterdam-born Peter Spier says he does not remember a time "when I did not dabble with clay, draw, or see someone draw . . ." His lively drawings in lovely colors, often filled with amusing details, are truly in the Caldecott tradition.

LYND WARD
The Biggest Bear   Houghton Mifflin
By the illustrator

Lynd Ward's illustrations are both strong and tender. Often they have a three-dimensional quality that is curiously effective. His use of color in such books as *Paul Revere* is beautiful, but no more so than his powerful black-and-whites. The homespun character of the people in *The Biggest Bear, Caldecott Medal, 1953,* the chubby appealing bear cub, and appalling size of the full-grown animal in contrast to small Johnny, and the lovely glimpses of the forest make this book one of Lynd Ward's masterpieces, both droll and beautiful.

GARTH WILLIAMS
A Brother for the Orphelines   Harper & Row
By Natalie Savage Carlson   In Great Britain: Blackie and Son
Illustration © 1959 by Garth Williams

Garth Williams' pictures add distinction to any book he illustrates. He works both in color and black and white, but whether he is illustrating a fantasy—*Charlotte's Web*—or historical fiction—the *Little House* books—or the inimitable French children in the *Orpheline* series, his touch is sure, and pictures and text are one. People or animals, character, mood, and situations are revealed with tenderness or humor: Wilbur, the "radiant" pig taking off from the top of the manure pile; or stubborn, gallant Josine with the foundling in the pousette, fleeing madly ahead of the National Bicycle racers, who bear down on her like an avalanche; or Josine and Mme. Flattot brooding tenderly over the baby. Garth Williams' pictures *are* the characters.

TARO YASHIMA
  Crow Boy   Viking
  By the illustrator

The theme of a timid little Japanese school boy at last finding a place
among his classmates is universal, as are so many of this author's
books about children: *Momo's Kittens, Umbrella,* and *The Youngest
One.* His lively illustrations are of Japanese children whether their
background is in their native land or the United States. *Crow Boy* is
especially appealing, both for its story and for the manner in which it
captures the atmosphere of a Japanese village and the surrounding
countryside.

MARGOT ZEMACH

Mommy, Buy Me A China Doll Farrar, Straus & Giroux
By Harve Zemach

This talented artist has illustrated more than thirty books for children, a number of which have received special honors. She has a special knack for seeing the droll and comic in human foibles and expresses these to perfection in her art work.

Title Index

*Numbers refer to individual entries, not to pages.

Author-Illustrator Index

*Numbers refer to individual entries, not to pages.